The Insurance Professional's Practical Guide to Workers' Compensation

The Insurance Professional's Practical Guide to Workers' Compensation

From History through Audit

Christopher J. Boggs

CPCU, ARM, ALCM, LPCS, AAI, APA, CWCA, CRIS, AINS

Contents

Chapter 1

Workers' Compensation History:
The Great Tradeoff!

Eighteenth century pirates and a nineteenth century German "Iron" Chancellor preceded the United States in the creation of a social system for the protection of injured workers. The modern workers' compensation system owes parts of its existence to this unique parentage.

Arrrrgh, I'm Hurt!

Pirates, contrary to popular myth, proved to be highly organized and entrepreneurial. Prior to their assignment to the ranks of outlaws, they were considered highly prized allies of the government; plundering and sharing the spoils with governors of the pre-Revolutionary colonies giving them a safe port.

Privateering (the gentlemen's term for piracy) was a dangerous occupation; taking booty away from those who did not want to give it up leads to sea battles, hand-to-hand combat and injury. Because of the ever-present chance of impairment, a system was developed to compensate injured "employees." There was one catch: he or she (there were female pirates, as well) had to survive the wounds to collect benefits as there was no recorded compensation for death.

Chapter 1 – Workers' Compensation History

Piratesinfo.com provides some information regarding the amount of payment made to the injured (payments were made in Spanish pieces of eight, which was a monetary unit used from about 1497 until 1869).

- Loss of an eye – 100 pieces of eight (about $96 in 2020)
- Loss of a finger – 100 pieces of eight (about $96 in 2020)
- Loss of left arm – 500 pieces of eight (about $480 in 2020)
- Loss of right arm – 600 pieces of eight (about $576 in 2020)
- Loss of left leg – 400 pieces of eight (about $386 in 2020)
- Loss of right leg – 500 pieces of eight (about $480 in 2020)

Average weekly wage for colonial Americans of this period equated to approximately two pieces of eight (about $1.92 in 2020) per week. Loss of an eye or finger would merit payment approximating 50 weeks of wages. The right arm was worth 300 weeks (a little less than six years). These compare rather closely to modern compensation schedules.

In addition to being compensated, injured crew members were allowed to remain on board and offered less strenuous duty. This was the creation of the first return-to-work program.

Marxism, Socialism and Workers' Compensation

Otto von Bismarck, the "Iron Chancellor," introduced Workers' Accident Insurance" in 1881. Phased in between 1881 and 1884, the program became the model for workers' compensation programs in Europe and ultimately America.

Bismarck was not known as a socially conscious ruler; the working conditions of the common man were not necessarily foremost in his mind. History teaches that his main concerns were the unification and growth of Germany (Prussia) and the protection of his position. But Bismarck's main political rivals were Marxists with socialist agendas (a feigned concern for the plight of the common man). On the top of this agenda was the creation of a social program for the protection of workers injured on the job, a workers' compensation program.

The "Iron Chancellor" eventually outlawed Marxist and other socialist-leaning parties, securing his rule. However, he did borrow some of their ideas to keep peace among the people. Workers' Accident Insurance became the first compulsory workers' compensation program enacted in a modern, industrialized Europe.

Austria followed Germany's lead, instituting a workers' compensation program in 1887. Norway joined the work comp revolution in 1894; and Finland instituted a workers' comp program in 1895.

The United Kingdom followed suit in 1897 by replacing the outdated Employer's Liability Act of 1880 with its own Workmen's Compensation Act. The employer's liability act was relatively expensive protection that depended on the court system. This is the same type of program common in America during the late nineteenth century and early twentieth century.

America and Workers' Compensation

America did not join the workers' compensation social revolution until the 1900s. Maryland (1902), Massachusetts (1908), Montana (1909) and New York (1910) each introduced workers' compensation statutes. All four laws were struck down under constitutional challenge as violating "due process."

New York's 1910 act faced fierce opposition from labor unions. Union officials feared that state control of worker benefits would reduce the need for and popularity of the union. With socialized care and compensation, they feared the necessity of the union was compromised and long-term loyalty to the union was in question.

On March 24, 1911, the New York Court of Appeals declared the state's compulsory workers' compensation law unconstitutional. One hundred forty-six (146) workers were killed the next day in a fire at the Triangle Waist Company in New York City. Not all were killed in the fire, most died attempting to escape the flames, jumping from nine and 10 stories up to the street below.

With no workers' compensation system, family members and dependents had to turn to the courts in an attempt to force Triangle to compensate the injured and the families of the dead. The owners were tried for manslaughter and acquitted. A civil suit against the owners netted each of 23 families $75 in damages (The Columbia Electronic Encyclopedia). New York finally adopted a workers' compensation law in 1913 that would withstand constitutional challenges.

Employer Negligence

Prior to the enactment of workers' compensation laws, the only source of compensation for any injured employee was through the courts. Employees had to prove the employer was negligent to gain any compensation for lost wages or medical bills. Employers utilized several defenses against charges of negligence:

- ***Assumption of Risk***: Proving negligence requires evidence that a duty of care is owed. When an employee assumes the risk of an inherently dangerous or recognizably potentially dangerous activity, the duty of care is lifted off the employer. With no required duty of care, there can be no negligence. Employees in hazardous occupations were believed to understand the hazards and assumed the risk of injury.

- ***Contributory Negligence***: This doctrine of defense states that if the injured person is even partially culpable in causing or aggravating his own injury, he is barred from any recovery from the other party. This is an absolute defense.

- ***Fellow Servant Rule***: Defense against employer negligence asserting that an employee's injury was caused by a fellow employee and not by the acts of the employer. If proven, negligence was not asserted against the employer and recovery could be severely limited or barred.

Very few workers had the means to bring suit. Those who could afford a lawsuit had to overcome the defenses available to the employer. The result: very few employers were held responsible for injury and required to pay. Awards for successful suits were unpredictable, ranging from too little to merit the trouble of filing suit to more than the employer planned to pay.

Congress enacted two laws to limit the harshness of these defenses. The Employers' Liability Acts of 1906 and 1908 were federal attempts to soften the contributory negligence doctrine. These legislative attempts did little to protect injured workers from the ravages of defense attorneys and juries.

The Great Tradeoff!

Human capital (the value of the employee) became a driving force behind the push for a system of protection. Stories (although no evidence currently exists) of injured mine workers being laid at the doors of their houses with no compensation or admission of negligence from the mine owners, leaving the families to struggle for a means of support and help, made their way through industrialized cities and states leading to demands for a better system. Recognition of the value of employees and other events between 1900 and 1911 helped spur the movement towards a social system of workers' compensation:

- **1908** – President Theodore Roosevelt signed the first viable workers' compensation statute into law with the creation of the Federal Employers Liability Act designed to protect railroad workers involved in interstate commerce (the program is still in existence today).

- **1908-1909** – Various states set up commissions to study the merits and drawbacks of a social system of injured employee compensation. Overwhelmingly these commissions reported that business, industry and employees supported such a system (the basis of study was the German law).

- **1910** – Crystal Eastman compiled and penned "Work Accidents and the Law." This document presented the problems inherent in the then-current system of negligence-based compensation in light of the cost to human capital. It also highlighted the benefits of a workers' compensation program as preventative in nature (employers would be more willing to invest in safety if the cost of injury was ultimately on them). This work is credited with changing businesses' and labor groups' attitudes towards workers' compensation and employee safety.

- **1911** – Triangle Waist Company fire (detailed above).

- **1911** – "The Great Tradeoff" debate. Before any plan could move forward, an agreement between labor and industry had to be reached; both had to be willing to give up something for a workers' compensation system to function properly. The employer agreed to pay medical bills and lost wages, regardless of fault; and the employee agreed to give up the right to sue.

Wisconsin passed its workers' compensation law in May 1911, becoming the first state to effectuate an ongoing workers' compensation program that survived legal challenges. Nine more states adopted workers' compensation laws before the close of 1911. By the end of 1920, 42 states plus Alaska and Hawaii (even though statehood didn't come for either until 1959) enacted workers' compensation statutes. Mississippi was the last state to implement a workers' compensation statute, waiting until 1948.

Voluntary vs. Compulsory

Early programs (1911-1916) were voluntary participation laws. Employers were not compelled by the various statutes to purchase workers' compensation. Compulsory participation laws had been found unconstitutional. The Fourteenth Amendment required due process before a person or entity could be compelled to part with property.

In 1917, the Supreme Court upheld the constitutionality of compulsory insurance requirements, opening up the doors for every state to require the purchase of workers' compensation coverage. Then, as now, each state instituted different threshold requirements.

Conclusion

Workers' compensation laws have evolved and expanded since the beginning, but these are the roots of the modern American workers' compensation system. The following chapters detail many of the issues surrounding workers' compensation rather than focusing merely on the coverage provided in the policy

Chapter 2

On-the-Job Injury:
The 'Course and Scope' Rule

Workers' compensation statutes differ among jurisdictions regarding the threshold for compulsory participation, benefit schedules, contractor/sub-contractor relationships and most other statutory specifics. But there is one concept on which every state agrees and to which every state subscribes. This point of agreement is that to be compensable, injury or illness must arise out of and in the course and scope of employment.

The Three Tests

"**Arising out of**..." indicates a causal connection between the furtherance of the employer's business and the injury. If the employer benefits in some way from the activity, then the injury or illness suffered in the pursuit of that activity is considered to "arise out of" the employment. One of three "causal connection" doctrines is applied by the various states.

- *Increased risk doctrine*. This is the most common among the jurisdictions. If the employment increases the chance of injury, then there is a causal connection between the work and the injury.

- ***Actual risk doctrine***. If the employment itself presents a risk of injury, then there is a causal connection between the employment and the injury.
- ***Positional risk doctrine.*** This is the minority view. Jurisdictions applying this test only require the injury occur at work to prove a causal connection between the work and the injury. The mere fact the person is at work is enough.

"In the course..." is a function of the timing and location of the injury or illness. The implication is that the injury must occur during operations for the employer, or "during employment," and at the employer's location or a location mandated or reasonably expected by the employer. New working conditions and relationships do not necessarily limit this to an on-site, 8-to-5 exposure.

Generally, if there is provable causal connection between the work and the injury (the "arising out of" test is satisfied), the "in the course of" test is also satisfied. However, the "in the course of" test is sometimes required to prove the injury arose out of the employment.

"Scope of employment..." test serves to more specifically define the first two tests by: 1) analyzing the motivations of the employee, 2) analyzing the employer's direction and control over the actions of the employee and 3) analyzing the employer's ability to foresee the activities of the employee. Employee actions which ultimately lead to an accident or injury must be motivated, in whole or in part, by the "desire" to further the interests of the employer. Motivation or desire can be out of fear that failure to perform will result in the loss of a job, or from a more altruistic desire to do well for the employer. The basis for the motivation or desire is irrelevant; it is the fact that the motivation exists that leads to compensability. Further, the actions must, to some extent, be at the presumed direction of the employer or potentially foreseen by the employer.

Injury may, in fact, arise out of and be in the course of employment but still be outside the scope of employment, negating compensability under workers' compensation law. For example, while entertaining clients, a company executive gets into an argument with a group sitting at another table because they are being too loud. A fight breaks out and the executive is severely injured. Such injury is not likely compensable under workers' compensation. Yes, the injury arose out of and in the course of employment (entertaining clients to further the employer's business), but was outside the scope of employment. The employer's goals were not furthered by the fight (nor was that the motivation), and the employer likely never directed nor foresaw the need for the employee to be involved in a fistfight as a result of his employment.

Another example of an injury outside the scope of employment can be found in Exhibit 2.1 at the end of this chapter. This recounts the story of a McDonald's employee shot after ejecting a patron from the restaurant.

Not Always Easy to Establish Course and Scope

Establishing an injury as work related is much simpler when employees work from a fixed place of employment on a fixed schedule and are injured while in the midst of their assigned duties. A production employee injured by a press (or whatever type of machine) during her shift will meet all three tests with only minor question. Likewise, an office employee injured when a computer falls on him raises little doubt that the injury arose out of and in the course and scope of employment. There are few objections that could be raised in these situations upon which a denial of coverage could be based (beyond drug use).

Employees away from the employer's premises, involved in employer-sponsored recreational activities, who like to horseplay or pull practical jokes on their coworkers, who have personal issues that leak over into work, or who have pre-existing conditions or a predisposition to injury present particular problems when judging the compensability of an injury. Injury to any employee falling into one of these categories requires careful evaluation before coverage is assured.

Have Briefcase/Tool Belt, Will Travel

Many employees travel to conduct business on behalf of their employer; injury suffered by an employee away from the premises for business purposes is generally considered to arise out of and in the course and scope of employment and is compensable. The proximate cause of the employee's injury is the furtherance of the employer's interest; that's the reason for such a broad extension of coverage for employees injured while travelling.

For example, a specialty electrical contractor is hired to install wiring at a plant several hundred miles away from the contractor's home office. The eight-man crew will be on site four days. Several hotel rooms are rented for the employees to stay in when the day's work is done. Every evening, the crew goes out to dinner; while walking to a restaurant next to the hotel, one employee steps in a hole, falls and breaks his arm. This is a compensable injury as he was still in the course and scope of his employment.

Under the application of "proximate cause," the employee would not have been walking through the parking lot to get dinner but for the fact that his employer sent him there to work. He is furthering the employer's business. Additionally, eating dinner is within the course and scope of the employment as the employer likely provided a stipend to pay for the meals, "directed" them to eat and could have reasonably foreseen them needing and wanting to eat.

After dinner, a member of the crew decides to drive over to visit some family and friends in the area. On his way back to the hotel he is badly injured in an at-fault automobile accident. Does the workers' compensation carrier have grounds to deny the compensability of the injury? Yes, payment for this injury will likely be denied. Visiting family and friends does not arise out of the employment and is not in the course and scope of the employment. The employer did not direct the employee to depart nor did he sanction the deviation from the approved path (job, hotel, dinner). This is considered abandonment of employment. The employee has undertaken a personal task/errand that neither benefits the employer, nor is approved by the employer.

Abandonment of employment is the point at which an employee deviates from the permitted or expected course and scope of the off-premises work and engages in activities not intended for the advancement of the employer's business nor directed by the employer. This includes any activity in direct contradiction to the rules, requests, or expectations of the employer.

Working from Home

Employees working from home-based offices are afforded the same workers' compensation protection as those camped in an office building. Determining the compensability for an injury suffered at home requires meeting the same qualifications as one suffered on site; injury must arise out of and in the course and scope of employment.

Tennessee's Supreme Court ruled on such a case in November 2007. InsuranceJournal.com reported the Court's findings in *Wait v. Travelers Indemnity Co. of Illinois* on November 26, 2007.

Kristina Wait took a lunch break from her work for the American Cancer Society; a neighbor knocked on her door and Wait let him inside. After a brief conversation the neighbor left but returned a few minutes later, claiming he forgot his keys, and brutally assaulted Wait upon re-entering the home.

Wait's claim for workers' compensation benefits was ultimately denied by the Tennessee Supreme Court. The court reasoned that while the kitchen was equivalent to an office-based lunch or break room and taking lunch was within normal course and scope of employment (expected and foreseen by the employer), the attack was outside the purview of workers' compensation because it had nothing to do with Wait's role for the ACS. It was simply a personally motivated attack unrelated to the employment.

Other Home-Based Problems

Another example of non-compensable injury might include a home-based employee taking a break to go attend to his children. He has abandoned his employment and is no longer pursuing the employer's interest, but his own. If he is injured while playing with the children, such injuries did not arise out of or in the course and scope of employment. If, however, a file cabinet topples over on him while searching for information, the injury is compensable.

Unique workers' compensation exposures are created for employers allowing employees to work from home; exposures that may not be present with office-based workers. These include greater exposure to road hazards, a change in the "coming and going" rule (detailed in Chapter 3) and difficulty meeting the requirement to provide a safe and healthy work environment.

For security and safety purposes or to provide a more professional appearance, employees with a home office may be directed or encouraged to set up a post office box or other mailbox arrangements rather than utilizing their home address. Having such a box requires the employee to check it periodically, unlike office-based employees whose mail is delivered to their desk or a central mail room. Traveling to and from the box is considered arising out of and in the course and scope of employment. Injury suffered in an auto accident may be a compensable injury.

Employers may allow certain employees to telecommute three or four days a week, requiring them to report to the office only once or twice a week for various reasons. Generally, workers' compensation benefits do not apply to employees travelling to and from work (known as the coming and going rule). However, since the employee is leaving one *per se* office location to travel to another, the entire trip may be considered in the course and scope of employment making any injury compensable.

Additional consideration must be given to telecommuting employees' health and safety. Employers are charged with providing a safe and healthy work environment; the requirement extends to employees working in their homes. Employers assure that employee workspace in the office is ergonomically designed, but rarely is such precaution taken with home-based employees. Repetitive motion injuries (such as carpel tunnel syndrome), back injuries from incorrect desk set-up and posture and eye strain are just as likely among telecommuting employees as among office-based staff. Employers are not on-site to risk manage and loss control the home office design, but workers' compensation claims from the same sorts of office-based injuries can still present themselves.

Exhibit 2.1

McDonald's Denial of Work Comp Benefits to Worker Shot is Appropriate

Nigel Haskett, 21 at the time he was shot, is or was an employee of a McDonald's franchise in Little Rock, Arkansas. On August 26, 2008, Haskett physically restrained a man and expelled him from the restaurant to end his battery of a female patron. Perry Kennon, the alleged attacker, went to his car, retrieved a gun and shot Haskett several times as he stood in front of the door to prevent Kennon's re-entry.

Police and the public have hailed Haskett's actions as heroic. But the franchisee's workers' compensation carrier is not swayed by such sentiment, they have denied Haskett's claim for workers' compensation benefits outright, claiming that his injuries did not "arise out of or within the course and scope of his employment" (as reported on rawstory.com and various other news sources).

The "Course and Scope" Rule

Few provisions surrounding workers' compensation coverage are agreed on by multiple states, much less every state. But every state does abide by the three-test "course and scope" rule. To be compensable, the injury must "arise out of and be in the course and scope of employment." Each of these terms is more specifically defined at the beginning of this chapter.

Comparing Haskett's Actions with the "Course and Scope" Tests

Do Haskett's actions meet the requirements of each test? Comparing his actions with each requirement will clarify whether the workers' compensation carrier is correct in its denial or not.

Arising out of...: Does protecting patron safety benefit the business and further the business' objectives? Haskett's attorney stated his belief in an interview with a Little Rock television station that these actions accomplished both. If it can be proven that the employer and the business did or would somehow benefit from Haskett's actions, his injury may be judged to have "arisen out of" his employment.

Presumably, McDonald's business objective is to prepare and serve food while maintaining a safe and clean environment for its employees and customers. The question of whether wrestling someone out of the restaurant to prevent them from attacking another person qualifies as being a part of that objective. If customers feel safe, they are likely to eat at the restaurant.

Although a definitive "yes" to the question of "arising out of..." is tough to give, Haskett's actions border on furthering the business' objectives. It appears that his being shot arose out of his employment and satisfies the first test.

In the Course of...: This test is much easier to assign a definitive "yes." Haskett was on the premises of his employer, he was "on the clock" and presumably working at the time (not on break). No question that the injury occurred during the course of his employment.

Scope of Employment: Compensability of Haskett's injury is on shaky ground when compared against the "scope of employment" test. This test has three qualifiers: 1) the motivation of the employee must be to further the employer's business, 2) the employer must have some direction and control over the employee's actions and 3) the situation and actions must be foreseeable by the employer.

- *Employee's motivation:* It is not likely that Haskett was motivated by the employer's business objectives. While his motivation was admirable, the protection of a seemingly defenseless individual, it does not meet the first test.

- *Direction and control of the employer*: While the employer, in a letter to the press, supports and applauds Haskett's dedicated actions, neither he nor any manager directed Haskett to act as he did. The second qualifier is also not met.

- *Employer's ability to foresee the situation and actions*: The question as to whether the situation was foreseen by the employer is somewhat gray based on the differing accounts provided by the two parties.

According to McDonald's, part of employee training and orientation is a directive to not "try to be a hero." The employee handbook specifically states that the police are to be called and the employee is to not engage a robber or other such individuals. Haskett states in news reports that he never received this training.

If such warning and direction is in the employee handbook, which probably contains a signed statement that it was read in its entirety by Haskett, then the employer did foresee the possibility for a dangerous situation and gave strict instruction for employees to not engage. It was the anticipation and instruction of the employer that the employee stay out of harm's way. The third qualifier also falls against Haskett and in favor of the workers' compensation carrier.

Haskett's injury was NOT in the "scope of employment." His actions met none of the three "scope" requirements and he fails the third test.

Not Compensable

Sadly, two-out-of-three is not good enough; all three "course and scope" tests must be passed. The workers' compensation carrier may be correct in their denial of workers' compensation benefits for this injury.

Some arguments for compensability of this injury say that Haskett would not have been injured "but for" his being at work; this argument falls short because workers' compensation is not solely based on proximate cause. Just being "at work" is not enough to garner protection.

Based on the letter of the law, this is not a compensable claim when compared to the three-test "course and scope" requirement. Perhaps Haskett and his attorney can show "implied consent" or "ratification" of his actions since the employer did not try to stop him from throwing Kennon out of the store; or pull him inside when he stood at the door to prevent the attacker's reentry. The employer's inaction may be considered "at the employer's direction."

Regardless, this will likely go to trial before it is finally settled. It is impossible to know what any jury will do, so stay tuned.

Chapter 3

Gray Areas in 'Course and Scope' Injuries

The threshold requirements that to be compensable an injury must: 1) arise out of, 2) be in the course of, and 3) be in the scope of employment leave many gray areas. Here are the major gray areas in the course and scope rules.

- The Coming and Going Rule
- "Forced Fun"
- Horseplay and Practical Jokes

'Coming and Going' Rule

Injury suffered traveling to work or home from work or even while going to and returning from lunch is generally not compensable. Known as the coming and going rule, the logic behind the rule is that the employee is not furthering the employer's interest or serving the business' needs. The employee is serving his own purposes and furthering his own cause during this course of travel; namely going to an employment situation where a paycheck is delivered for services rendered, going to lunch or going home.

The employer is not the proximate cause of the individual being on the road. The employee has not arrived at a place where services are rendered to the employer and injury suffered is not compensable.

Exceptions to the coming and going rule do exist. Anytime travel is an integral part of employment or such travel furthers the employer's business, the coming and going rule is superseded, making injury compensable. Travel considered integral to the employment includes travel between jobsites and travel to meet clients.

Other "special hazard" exceptions to the coming and going rule include:

- ***Employer-furnished transportation.*** If the employer undertakes to provide group transportation to and from office or job site, injury suffered during the trip is compensable. An off-beat example, especially in areas where there is little snow, is the small business owner who picks up his/her employees on snowy days to assure the office is staffed and, altruistically, to keep the employees from having to drive. Employee injury during this travel is potentially compensable under workers' compensation.

- ***The employee performs a beneficial errand for the employer.*** Going to the bank, the post office or on any other errand to further the business of the employer qualifies as a beneficial errand. If the errand requires the employee to deviate from her normal route, any injury suffered from the time the employee leaves the premises until she returns to her normal route is likely compensable. Errands taking the employee outside his normal ways and means are considered "for the benefit" of the employer making injury compensable.

- ***Injury suffered by an "on call" employee.*** Doctors or those in other employments who must be ready to respond when the "call" comes are considered to be within the course and scope of employment immediately upon responding to the call. The drive is considered to be part of furthering the employer's business making injury compensable.

- ***If the employer reimburses or pays the employees*** transportation costs, the trip is considered business-related and for the benefit of the employer. Injury suffered is compensable unless abandonment of employment is proven.

- ***Injury suffered once the employee enters the parking lot.*** Courts ascribe a reasonable time for employees to reach their assigned workstation. During this time, the employee is considered to be in the course and scope of employment. "The clock" begins to tick (so to speak) when the employee arrives in the parking lot. The reverse is true; the employee is considered to be within course and scope until he leaves the parking lot. Injury suffered prior to and after leaving the parking lot is not covered (unless one of the other exceptions apply). The breadth of this special exception is applied differently by each state.

Play Ball! Or 'Forced Fun'

Extending the "course and scope of employment" doctrine to recreational activities combines questions of fact decided by juries and questions of law decided by the court. Employees injured while participating in recreational activities while on the employer's premises or at the employer's direction may qualify for workers' compensation coverage. Four tests are applied to the facts surrounding the injury to decide compensability.

1. ***Did the accident occur on the employer's premises?*** An affirmative response does not guarantee compensability. An employee injured while engaged in a pick-up basketball game on the employer's premises will not be eligible for workers' compensation because the employer is not directly benefitting from the activity nor is the employer directing the activity. Making recreational facilities available does not make the employer liable. But neither is it required that the injury occur on the employer's premises to be compensable.

2. ***Was the event or team organized by the employer?*** Company-organized softball teams competing in "industrial leagues" may qualify under this provision. However, several employees deciding to form a team is wholly different from a team organized by the employer, encouraging "good" ballplayers to participate.

3. ***Did the employer pay for the activity?*** It is unclear if this refers to the total cost or a subsidy on behalf of the team. For example, the league charges every player $50 but the company pays $40 on behalf of each player/employee. While the activity is not fully paid for by the employer, it could be viewed as an employer-paid or sponsored (with participation encouraged).

4. ***Did the employer benefit?*** Advertising in the community (team shirts), improved employee morale or better teamwork. An employer can "benefit" from these activities in more ways than tangible outputs.

Employee picnics, team building outings and Christmas dinners are a few examples of other types of recreational and social activities that may lead to compensable injuries. State statutes should be reviewed regarding the issue of recreational activities. Some states have adopted relative pro-employer statutes to limit compensability to activities in which employees are expected to participate.

Horseplay and Practical Jokes

Court and legislative attitudes have shifted regarding the compensability of injury suffered as a result of horseplay. Historically courts held that horseplay was such a deviation from the course and scope of employment as to qualify as an abandonment of duty. Injury suffered outside the "course and scope" is not eligible for workers' compensation protection;

injured employees, even the non-participating (innocent) party, were routinely denied coverage.

"We are clearly convinced here that our old rule should be abandoned. Although appropriate for the time in which it arose, we are persuaded by the overwhelming weight of contrary authority in our sister states and current legal commentary." With this statement, the Kansas Supreme Court overturned decades of prior case law regarding compensability of injury resulting from horseplay. The court's opinion in Coleman v. Armour Swift-Eckrich mirrors the prevailing attitude surrounding injury arising out of horseplay; especially injury to the non-participating/innocent employee that such injury could still fall within the course and scope of employment.

Prevailing opinion now centers on and applies a treatise known as "Larson's Workers' Compensation Law" (Larson). Larson applies a four-part test of the facts surrounding the horseplay-associated injury to establish compensability.

- The extent and seriousness of the deviation. Was the horseplay "reasonable" or did the parties go so far out of the way as to constitute unreasonable deviation? In one case, three men wrapped another employee from his ankles to his shoulders in duct tape. The injured employee was allowed to forego the sole remedy offered by workers' compensation and sue the participants in tort as the activities were considered too far outside "normal."

- The completeness of the deviation. Was the horseplay comingled with the regular performance of duties or did it involve (and require) an abandonment of duty?
- The extent to which the practice of horseplay has become an accepted part of the employment. If horseplay, practical jokes and hazing are common and not discouraged or forbidden by the employer, then it is reasonably judged to be part of normal employment and within course and scope.
- The extent to which the nature of employment may be expected to include some horseplay. Some industries lend themselves to horseplay; those working in those industries should expect to be exposed to it. As such, it is a normal part of employment and injury may be compensable.

According to Larson itself, it is not required that all four tests be satisfied for an injury to be compensable. "It is now clearly established that the nonparticipating victim of horseplay may recover compensation."

Chapter 4

Occupational Disease and Workers' Compensation Protection

Occupational diseases cause 860,000 illnesses and 60,300 deaths in the United States annually, according to the American Academy of Family Physicians. Illness directly attributable to work conditions and exposures is diagnosed in approximately 10 percent of hospitalized patients.

Judged against the standard that to be compensable an injury or illness must arise out of and in the course and scope of employment, rarely do employers or even employees view an illness as clearly crossing the required threshold. Qualifying an illness as a compensable occupational disease often requires industrial commission or court intervention. Occupational disease claims can be further complicated, in the legal sense, by environmental factors, personal habits, pre-existing conditions and the individual's medical history.

To be considered "occupational" and therefore compensable, the disease must arise out of or be caused by conditions peculiar to the work. Black lung disease (coal workers' pneumoconiosis (CWP) or anthracosis) results from prolonged exposure to coal dust in higher-than-normal concentrations, making the disease peculiar to the coal mining industry. Another example of a compensable occupational disease peculiar to an industry is a healthcare worker contracting an infectious disease such as HIV or hepatitis as a result of exposure to and contact with infected blood.

Sources of Occupational Disease

Conditions attributable to occupational exposure cover the gamut of common and uncommon illnesses, making it all the more difficult to connect the dots between the illness or injury and the course and scope of employment. Injuries commonly connected to work conditions include: carpal tunnel syndrome (and other repetitive-motion type injuries), hearing loss (when around noisy operations), black lung disease, asbestosis, silicosis, contact dermatitis and even Lyme disease contracted by employees working in wooded areas.

Some illnesses less clearly attributable to work-related exposure include the following.

- *Asthma*: Usually affects employees working with animal and plant products, wood dust, metals such as cobalt, cutting oils and irritants such as sulfur dioxide.
- *Bronchitis*: Common among employees working around high concentrations of acids, smoke and nitrogen oxides.
- *Hypersensitivity pneumonitis*: Most often found in workers around moldy hay and cutting oils (common among farming and agricultural operations; may want to recommend coverage to farms without the requisite number of employees).

- **Respiratory irritation and infections**: Affects mainly office workers arising out of indoor air pollution (a.k.a. sick building syndrome).
- **Liver cancer**: Generally results from exposure to vinyl chloride common in plastics manufacturing.
- **Bladder cancer**: Found in employment exposed to benzidine (common in plastics and chemical manufacturing).
- **Skin cancer**: Common in workers with long-term exposure to ultraviolet light (i.e. landscapers, construction workers, etc.).
- **Brain and other tumors**: May be the result of employee's long-term exposure to radiation.
- **Spontaneous abortion**: Often results from exposure to ethylene oxide.
- **Sperm abnormalities**: Can result from exposure to dibromochloropropane commonly used in the manufacture of pesticides.
- **Birth defects**: Usually the result of exposure to ionizing radiation (may open the employer to an Employers' Liability claim).
- **Coronary artery disease**: Mostly attributable to employees exposed to carbon monoxide and stressful working conditions.
- **Neurologic disorders**: Nervous system disorders are generally the result of employee exposure to toxins, organic solvents, metals and pesticides. Prolonged exposure or exposure to a high concentration of these

substances can cause headaches, fatigue, cognitive disorders and even depression.

- ***Parkinson's disease***: Associated with employment exposed to carbon monoxide poisoning and/or chronic exposure to manganese fumes or dust.
- ***Stress-related illnesses***: Heart attacks, stroke and other like injuries will be explored below.
- ***Eye and sight problems***: Office-bound employees often experience eye and sight problems due to the need to focus on a computer screen for long periods.

Medicine and the Courts

Classifying an illness as an occupational disease making it compensable under workers' compensation requires the combination of medical opinion and testimony and a legal finding of fact. Each case is judged on its own merits and encompassing circumstances, thus there is no singular test that can be applied to every case to declare the illness as compensable or non-compensable.

Medical opinion leading to the conclusion that an illness is work-related is not necessarily based on the disease but on the facts surrounding the patient's sickness. Physicians will investigate certain facts.

- The timing of the symptoms in relation to work: Do symptoms worsen at work and improve following prolonged absence from work (in the evening and on weekends)?

- Co-workers showing similar symptoms: Do co-workers show some of the same symptoms currently or in the past (may not be to the same degree as the patient as each individual has varying tolerances)?

- If such illness is common to employees in that particular industry.

- If the employee has a predisposition that may lend itself to the illness such as an allergy.

- Personal habits and medical history of the patient: Patients in poor medical condition (overweight, smokers, unrelated heart disease, etc.) and poor family medical histories may be more likely to contract a disease or illness than others in similar circumstances would not, clouding the relationship between the occupation and the illness. For example, smokers may be ill-equipped to fight off the effects of chemical concentrations to which others may have no problem being exposed.

Industrial commissions and courts: 1) compile the opinion of the treating physician and the opinions of other expert medical witnesses, 2) couple the medical evidence with the facts surrounding the case and 3) compare the subject case with precedent to render a compensability ruling. This process can sometimes take years.

Stress-Related Illness

Establishing an illness as work-related is difficult even with ample evidence to show a causal connection between the exposures applicable to the position and the contracted disease. It is made more difficult when the cause of the illness leading to bodily injury is a factor as intangible as stress.

Stress is most commonly pulled into occupational injury claims when the employee is seeking compensation for a heart attack, stroke or other related cardiovascular injuries. Case law surrounding the compensability of a stress-induced heart attack is less than consistent.

Tennessee's Supreme Court provided some relevant guidance regarding the compensability of stress-related injury in its March 2007 *Lane v. City of Cookeville* ruling. After considering the disparate medical evidence and the facts surrounding the heart attack Lane suffered allegedly due to the stress related to his police detective role, the court ruled that Lane's heart attack was not the result of any extraordinary stress and subsequently denied his petition for permanent total disability benefits.

The court declared in this ruling that a heart attack is compensable if caused by the worker's physical exertion or by mental or emotional stimulation. The stimulation would have to result from a specific acute or sudden stressful event rather than a generalized condition of stress. Presumably, a long buildup of stress would not fall into the compensable category.

Other published court findings and general rules of thumb require that the stress be of an unusual or abnormal nature, not stress that would be common to a certain job.

Which Policy Responds?

Occupational illnesses generally have a long gestation period. Employees may be exposed to the harmful condition for many years before the illness manifests. It is also possible that the employee doesn't contract the disease until years after the exposure ends.

The workers' compensation policy specifically states that the policy in effect at the employee's last exposure responds to the illness – even if the employee is working for another employer at the time the disease manifests itself.

Conclusion

Occupational disease resulting in bodily injury tends to lend itself to litigation. Since there is rarely a definable place or time of the injury, industrial commissions and courts will likely continue to play a large role in these claims.

Employees' personal habits and medical histories will, likewise, continue to find their way into the piles of evidence as workers' compensation carriers look for legitimate ways to deny coverage. Employees who are overweight (or even obese), with high blood pressure and who smoke will likely have to prove that those conditions in no way contributed to the work-related heart attack for which they are seeking benefits.

Employees contracting cancer from long-term exposure to radiation may see carriers digging into their medical history to find a family history of cancer.

Not to blame or accuse, but the nature of occupational disease claims will see and has seen both extremes in court.

Chapter 5

Benefits Provided Under Workers' Compensation Laws

Injuries or illnesses established as compensable under applicable workers' compensation law require prescribed benefits be paid to the injured employee. Benefit limits and duration vary by jurisdiction, but each state provides essentially the same three "classes" of benefits.

- Medical benefits
- Disability/Indemnity benefits
- Death Benefits

Medical Benefits

Medical benefits are usually unlimited with no deductible. Payments are made to the point that the injured employee is cured and/or given maximum relief. Bills for service go directly to the workers' compensation carrier and payment is made directly to the healthcare provider; the employee's only responsibility is to follow the doctor's orders.

Although the medical care provided, and the billing, are handled exclusively by the treating physician and the workers' compensation carrier, states differ regarding physician choice. Twenty-one states require the employee to use the physician picked by the employer from among a list of "authorized" physicians. The twenty-nine remaining states plus the District of Columbia allow the employee to choose the physician, with some requiring periodic consultation with an insurer-chosen physician. But nineteen of the "employee-choice" states limit the employee's options to physicians within a managed care type network.

Basic medical benefits are treated the same in every state. All statutes require medical costs, surgical fees, nursing care expense and medication costs necessary to "effect a cure and give relief" be fully paid by the workers' compensation insurer. Additional medical benefits are the same in every state, but with jurisdictional nuances. Rehabilitative services are a prime example. Every state provides some form of rehabilitation benefit, but not necessarily to the same extent or in the same amount.

Rehabilitative service benefits can include medical rehabilitation, vocational rehabilitation and psychological rehabilitation. Some states include the cost of rehabilitation services within the auspices of the medical benefits making coverage unlimited, where other states provide a sub-limit in the form of a dollar amount (as a specific benefit limit or based on the percentage of disability) or as a time limit (maximum number of weeks or visits, etc.).

Qualifying for rehabilitation services benefits requires the employee suffer "catastrophic injury" as defined by each state. Generally, a "catastrophic injury" requires some form of permanence. Rehabilitation services benefits pay the following, subject to any applicable sub limits.

- The cost of occupational rehabilitation necessary to return to maximum mobility and performance the injury will allow.
- The cost for necessary modifications to the employee's home allowing for maximum self-sufficiency.
- The cost for modifications to the employee's vehicle, such as the cost to affix a wheelchair lift, etc.
- The cost to modify the employee's workspace if able to return to work at the same employer.

If the employee is unable to return to work with his previous employer due to the unavailability of an accommodating position or the inability to offer a job to accommodate the employee's limitations, vocational rehabilitation benefits are extended to cover certain costs.

- The costs of aptitude and interest tests to customize an education/training program to the employee.
- The costs necessary for the employee to learn new skills or enhance existing skills.
- The cost necessary to provide job search and interview skills.
- The cost of job placement services.

Travel expenses to and from medical treatments are also paid under the medical benefit. Some states reimburse all mileage driven in the pursuit of medical treatment for work-related injury; others require the mileage to exceed a certain threshold (North Carolina requires the round trip to be greater than 20 miles before mileage is reimbursed).

Disability/Indemnity Benefits

Injured employees may be totally unable to work or to garner the same pay as was earned prior to the injury, subjecting them to either a complete loss of income or a diminished lifestyle. Medical benefits coverage pays any and all medical bills arising out of an occupational injury or illness, but loss of income is a separate benefit paid at the direction of and in amounts mandated by workers' compensation statutes.

Disability/indemnity benefits are subject to statutory minimum and maximum weekly payments, a maximum period of payments and/or a maximum amount of payments. These statutorily defined limits are based on the severity of the injury and the expected term (length) of the resulting condition.

Injury severity is classified as either partial or total. The term of the injury is assigned to either temporary or permanent status. Benefit payments are based on the combination of these conditions as per the following examples.

- **Temporary Partial:** Defines an injury from which the employee is expected to completely recover in some period of time with no or only minor long-term effects. A broken arm is an example if this type of injury. Employees suffering temporary partial injuries can generally return to work under "light-duty" assignments until the "temporary" condition heals. Benefits for employees within this category of injury include medical benefits, lost wages and/or differential pay if income is lower due to light-duty assignment.

- **Temporary Total:** A full recovery from the injury is expected, but for a period of time the employee is completely unable to work due to the injury. These types of injuries might require bed rest or hospitalization while the employee heals. All medical bills are paid as are lost wages subject to minimum and maximum amounts once any required waiting period (discussed below) has been satisfied. Duration of benefits: Thirty-three states pay temporary total disability benefits for the duration of the disability; one limits payment to the point of "maximum medical improvement;" and the rest cut off payment at a specified number of weeks ranging between 104 and 500 weeks.

- **Permanent Partial:** The employee has suffered an injury from which he will never recover, but one that will not prevent him from returning to some type of work. Amputation of a finger or leg and the loss of an eye or ear are examples of this injury classification. Benefits paid include all medical costs, statutorily scheduled benefits based on the injury (i.e. 40 weeks for the loss of a thumb) and potentially rehabilitative service benefits. Duration of benefits: Nine states pay for the duration of the disability (which seems unusual since it is "permanent"); six limit payment to 500 weeks; three base the length of benefit payments on the percentage of impairment; and the remainder limit payment to a specified number of weeks ranging between a low of 200 weeks to a high of 1,500 weeks (almost 29 years).

- **Permanent Total:** Recovery is not predicted; the employee is not expected to ever be able to return to work. Benefits paid will include medical bills to maximum cure and/or relief and lost wages. Duration of benefits: Although the injury is permanent and total, disability benefits are not necessarily paid for life. Many states pay for the "duration of the disability," others specify that payment is for the rest of the injured employee's life. A few states end benefits at specified ages; some end payment at "age 65," others at "age 67" or some at "retirement age." Two of the more restrictive states limit payment to 400 or 500 weeks and one state limits total disability benefits to $125,000.

Benefit payments are calculated based on the employee's "average weekly wages" (AWW) for the most recent 12-month period and are limited by minimum and maximum benefit amounts. Injured employees whose AWW is below the maximum limit still do not receive 100 percent of their average weekly wage during the period of disability, rather they receive a percentage of the AWW specified by the state. Two reasons benefits are lower than the employee's AWW are: 1.) benefits are not taxable; and 2.) to encourage injured employees to return to work — a moral hazard is created when the employee makes just as much out of work as he does while at work. Most states pay two-thirds (66 2/3 percent) of the employee's average weekly wage, but the benefit ranges anywhere between 60 percent and 80 percent of the employee's AWW. Disability benefits are usually adjusted annually to account for inflation and expected changes in income.

Maximum disability benefits are based on a percentage of the statewide average weekly wage (SAWW) across all industries. For example, one state bases its maximum average weekly wage benefit on 200 percent of the state's average weekly wage; where several other states use 66 2/3 percent of the state's average weekly wage to limit its maximum benefit. All other states fall somewhere in this range.

Injured employees must satisfy waiting periods before they are eligible to receive disability/indemnity benefits. "Elimination periods" range between three and seven days with each state incorporating a retroactive provision allowing the elimination period to be indemnified should the period of disability exceed a specified threshold. North Carolina, for example, has a seven-day waiting period before disability benefits are paid; however, if the period of disability goes beyond 21 days, the policy goes back and retroactively indemnifies the employee for the first seven days, effectively providing coverage from the date of injury.

Although workers' compensation is a no-fault system intended to be the sole remedy, there are activities in which employees can participate that can potentially eliminate or reduce disability benefits. Employees who intentionally inflict injury on themselves or whose injury can be directly attributable to the use or abuse of alcohol or drugs may see their disability benefits eliminated. Employees in some states who fail to wear required safety equipment risk seeing their benefits reduced by a specified percentage.

Death Benefits

Death benefits are the last of the three benefit classes dictated by workers' compensation statutes, this extends a limited amount towards funeral expenses plus a weekly benefit to eligible dependents. To collect death benefits from the workers' compensation policy: 1) death must occur within a certain period of time following the work-related injury to be considered a work-related death and 2) a request for death benefits must be made within a specified period following death (to avoid long-tail death claims).

Funeral/burial expense benefits vary widely across the country. The national funeral expense benefit average is a little more than $5,200. Mississippi provides the lowest benefit at $2,000, while Minnesota has the highest at $15,000.

Dependent benefits are also limited by statute. Some states pay benefits based on the employee's average weekly wages for the remainder of the surviving spouse's life, others limit payment to a specified number of weeks. Provisions in other states pay until the spouse remarries or until a certain dollar amount is paid; there is truly no "standard" provision regarding spouses.

Benefits paid to or for surviving children are somewhat more uniform. Most states pay some specified amount until the child is 18. Some states provide additional benefits based on the child's education or ability status.

Death benefits, like the other workers' compensation benefits, are not nationally uniform so individual state laws must be studied to completely understand the specific state allowances.

Conclusion

Every state pays basic medical benefits essentially uniformly. However, each state takes a different path towards the satisfaction of additional medical benefits, disability benefits and death benefits. Resource information can be found on each state's workers' compensation/industrial commission Web site, from the Bureau of Labor Statistics (BLS) and on the AFLCIO Web site.

Chapter 6

Second Injury Funds: Are They Still Necessary or Just a Drain On the System?

Second (or subsequent) injury funds (SIFs) have been abolished in 19 states. Alabama and Maine began this movement in 1992, with Arkansas and New York being the most recent converts; each ending its respective program in 2007. Some states, such as South Carolina, have already passed laws that call for the end of their second injury funds over the next several years. Further, the American Insurance Association has been at war against second injury funds since at least the mid-1990s, working to convince the remaining states to abolish or substantially alter the fund programs that still exist. Appendix "B" lists the status of second injury funds for all states.

Has the time for second injury funds passed? Are these archaic social programs that have outlived their usefulness? It depends on who is being asked and that party's agenda. Regardless of which side is making the argument, the focus is on money: the cost if the plan is kept intact or the cost if the plan is abolished. It is all about the money, regardless of the eloquence of any other presented reason.

In the search for answers to these questions, the next few paragraphs will provide a bit of SIF program history, the threshold for protection, benefits offered, how the funds are financed and conclude with arguments for and against dismantling this decades-old employer safety net.

History of Second Injury Funds

New York created the nation's first Second Injury Fund in 1916, just three years after creation of its workers' compensation statute. Few states followed suit until World War II with most states adopting second injury funds in the early-to-mid 1940s based around a model national code. The rush to provide this employer protection was created by the desire to clear the path for veterans who had sustained injury during the war. Injured veterans were not being hired due to employers' fears of being held financially responsible for the cumulative effect of an on-the-job injury coupled with a pre-existing war injury. Second injury funds were designed to temper if not completely remove this fear.

Employers' fears were cultivated by several court cases culminating in a 1925 Oklahoma Supreme Court ruling, *Nease v. Hughes Stone Co.* This proved to be a landmark case regarding an employer's liability for an employee's injuries which synergistically compound a pre-existed condition.

W.A. Nease was already blind in one eye when he began work for Hughes Stone Company. During his employment, an explosion destroyed Nease's remaining eye, leaving him blind and permanently and totally disabled. The employer through the insurance carrier provided 100 weeks of indemnity payments as was required by statutory provisions governing the loss of one eye. Nease argued that since he was permanently disabled, not merely partially disabled, he was due lifetime benefits. The Oklahoma Supreme Court agreed, awarding him lifetime benefits and making the employer and the insurer responsible for total disability indemnity benefits.

A U.S. Labor Department report stated that between 7,000 and 8,000 one-eyed, one-legged and one-handed men in Oklahoma lost their jobs immediately following this ruling. Employers did not want to take the chance of being held financially responsible for an employee's total disability. A mechanism to relieve employers of this responsibility was required. Second injury funds were created to remedy the problems and accomplish two goals.

1. Encourage employers to hire and retain workers with pre-existing injuries or conditions.
2. Provide economic relief to employers for an employee's subsequent injury.

Threshold Requirements to Receive Benefits

Not every injury suffered by an individual with a pre-existing injury or condition is compensable under the second injury funds still in operation. Certain requirements must be met before any benefits are payable from these funds. States differ on the application of SIF compensability requirements, but each applies the following requirements to varying degrees.

- There must be a prior injury that is a hindrance or obstacle to employment. Some states allow the prior injury to emanate from any cause while others require the prior injury to be work-related. It is not necessary for successive injuries to be to the same or a similar body part to be eligible for SIF protection.

- There must be a pre-existing medical condition that affects employment such as epilepsy, diabetes, Parkinson's disease, arthritis and others found in a list of 34 to 37 different conditions. Some states consider the list of conditions an "exclusive list," meaning that only listed conditions are eligible for second injury fund protection; other states consider this a "presumptive list" meaning that those listed are the only ones presumed to require second injury protection, but compensable conditions are not limited to the list allowing others to be submitted for consideration.

- The prior injury or condition must be diagnosed and documented by the employer before the second injury occurs. Massachusetts is the only state that places a time limit as to when the employer must know about the pre-existing condition; employers must document the pre-existing condition within 30 days of hire before any subsequent injury is eligible for second injury fund protection. Other states only require that the condition be known and documented before the subsequent injury. This documentation can be as simple as a letter in the employee's file noting the condition. This is a potentially tricky situation due to the Americans with Disabilities Act (ADA) and what employers can and cannot ask or do. These conditions can be discovered and documented as a result of a post-hire physical or a medical condition questionnaire completed by the employee. Attorneys should be consulted regarding the legalities surrounding this requirement and how the data can be gathered without violating ADA or other laws.

- A few states require the prior injury to be classified as a permanent partial disability.
- Some states require a certain percentage of impairment; and others only pay if the second injury results in permanent total disability.
- The fund must be put on notice when an employee with a pre-existing condition is injured; regardless if it is known whether or not benefits are going to be requested.
- A waiting period must be satisfied during which time the primary workers' compensation carrier pays all disability/indemnity benefits. The waiting period can range between 52 and 104 weeks.

Benefits Offered by Second Injury Funds

Second injury fund states operate as either "reimbursement funds" or "take-over funds" to pay benefits owed to qualifying employees. Reimbursement fund states operate on the principle that the best and most efficient mechanism for handling on-going injury claims is the continued involvement of the insurance carrier or self-insured employer's third party administrator (TPA); these states reimburse the insurance carrier or self-insurer for all payments made to employees qualifying for protection. Take-over fund states, as the name suggests, remove the injured employee from the primary workers' compensation system and take over payment of disability/benefits, removing the insurance carrier or self-insured employer from the process.

Every state SIF pays qualifying employees the difference between the injury suffered and the cumulative effect of the trauma. Using the *Nease* ruling presented above as an example, had a second injury fund existed the primary insurer would have only been required to pay the 100 weeks for the loss of an eye and the second injury fund would have taken over and paid all disability benefits due an individual with a permanent total disability.

Benefits offered by some but not all states include the following (not an all-inclusive list).

- **Lost wages from a second job held by the employee.** States providing this benefit reason that if the employee holds two jobs (presumably for needed extra money), then the permanent total disability not only prevents him from working his primary job but also prevents his working a second job, thus a percentage of those lost wages are also paid.

- **Primary workers' compensation benefits for uninsured workers**. A few states extend their second injury fund to provide primary workers' compensation benefits to injured employees of employers that did not purchase workers' compensation coverage.

- **Continued disability payments when state-mandated benefits end.** Some states limit permanent total disability benefits to a specified number of weeks; second injury funds in a few of those states pick up and continue benefits for injured employees that "outlive" the benefit period. Indiana, for example, limits permanent total disability benefits to 500 weeks; if the injured employee is still alive, the second injury fund picks up and provides continued benefits in 150-week increments.

Financing Second Injury Funds

Second injury funds are most commonly financed by insurer assessments, employers and/or self-insured funds. These assessments can be in the form of a required dollar amount per claim or a percentage of each specified type of claim. These percentages generally range between 2.5 percent to 6 percent or more.

Statutes often specify the injuries that must be assessed. North Carolina, for example, requires a $250 assessment for all losses that result in the "loss, or loss of use, of each minor member in every case of a permanent partial disability where there is such loss;" and $750 "for 50 percent or more loss, or loss of use of each major member, defined as back, foot, leg, hand, arm, eye, or hearing."

Funding is sometimes provided by death benefits owed to an employee with no legal heirs. The death benefit that was due to the employee is put into the second injury fund. In fact, this is Texas' sole means of financing its second injury fund.

The Decline of Second Injury Funds

Second (subsequent) injury funds (SIFs) represent socialized care requiring that the large group of insurers, self-insurers and, in some states, employers subsidize the few. This is one bullet in the revolver used by the American Insurance Association (AIA) and other anti-SIF groups to shoot at the remaining second injury funds.

There are two other charges leveled against the remaining funds by the anti-SIF groups.

- The Americans with Disabilities Act (ADA) makes these funds obsolete. SIFs are no longer necessary because the ADA prohibits discrimination against disabled workers provided: 1) the employer has 15 or more employees; 2) the job can be performed if only "reasonable accommodations" are made; and 3) the accommodations do not create an undue hardship on the employer.
- Second injury funds have failed to meet the objective of promoting the hiring of disabled workers.

It's an intriguing combination of charges. If ADA laws made the funds obsolete, then the SIFs no longer have to make promoting the hiring of disabled workers a priority. Now these funds can focus on the more important goal of being a safety net for employers now *required* by law to hire disabled workers.

One trade association attorney stated it best when she conceded that the ADA did effectively replace the first goal of second injury funds. She went on, however, to make the point that while the ADA created a legal requirement to assist the disabled, it did nothing to help employers bound by the law secure financing for any additional costs that may be created if and when an employee with a pre-existing medical condition is permanently and totally disabled because of the cumulative effects of a workplace injury. Should employers forced to hire disabled workers also be saddled with additional costs over which they have no control, such as higher costs resulting from an increased experience modification factor and/or the possible loss of premium credits due to more expensive claims?

Many view the experience modification factor argument as fallacious since experience mods are weighted more towards frequency than severity (with severe claims subject to a "stop gap" amount). Such a counterargument is true, unless the insured is in a state's assigned risk program, making the insured subject to an Assigned Risk Adjustment Program (ARAP) factor. ARAP factor calculations give greater weight to severity than do NCCI or state workers' compensation rating bureaus. Short of being in the assigned risk plan, the lack of a second injury fund may be inconsequential in the effect on experience modification factors.

Other arguments for the dissolution of second injury funds made by anti-SIF groups include the following.

- They deviate from the principle that an employer's costs should be internalized. All costs of doing business should be on the employer regardless of their part in creating the cost. Workers' compensation itself is a cost of doing business and all costs associated with providing this social benefit, including the costs of cumulative traumas, should be paid by the employer; with the ultimate cost being passed to the consumer rather than other employers or insurers. Anti-SIF groups argue than any increase in the cost of coverage will be more than negated by lower premiums due to the absence of carrier assessments (ultimately paid as part of the premium anyway). This leads to the next objection to second injury funds.

- Most second injury funds have accumulated large unfunded deficits.

- Second injury funds carry a large administrative cost.

- SIF disputes promote attorney involvement, further increasing the cost of second injury funds specifically and workers' compensation coverage in general.

- Some states extend benefits to employees whose employer failed to secure workers' compensation coverage either because they were not required to by law or they violated the law mandating they buy it. This may be a misuse of assessed funds; employers who break the law should not be bailed out by every other employer and insurance carrier operating within the law. Certainly no one wants the injured employee to go without care or benefits, but this is not part of the original intent of these funds. The injured employee has the court system and other government social programs from which to garner benefits.

- Most states require the employer to know about and have noted in the employee's file any pre-existing condition in order to qualify for second injury fund protection. Due to modern employment law and privacy concerns, such questioning may be considered an invasion of the employee's right to privacy regarding his health. Navigating these waters just to qualify for second injury fund protection could be hazardous.

Second injury funds are quickly losing favor and being legislated out of existence. Nineteen have disappeared since 1992 (incidentally, the year that the ADA was passed) and at least one more dissolved by 2013. Have these funds outlived their usefulness? There appear to be more arguments for closing these funds than for their continuation.

Chapter 7
Who Qualifies as an 'Employee' in Workers' Compensation Law?

Workers' compensation is compulsory in all states except Texas. Texas' coverage is compulsory for some contractor classifications. Although requirements vary, every compulsory and pseudo-compulsory state mandates that "employers" with a specified number of "employees" provide workers' compensation benefits either through the purchase of a workers' compensation policy, as a qualified self-insurer or out of pocket.

Thirty-six states and the District of Columbia require any entity with one employee or more to provide workers' compensation benefits; only 14 states allow employers to have more than one employee before protection is required (these thresholds range between three and five employees). Sounds simple, except that this calculation is complicated by each state's definition of "employee;" the definition hinges on how the person is engaged to do the work and the employer's legal structure.

'Employee?'

"Employee" is generally defined as a person hired to perform certain services or tasks for particular wages or salary under the control of another (the employer); or a worker hired to perform a specific job usual and customary to the employer's business operation in exchange for money or other remuneration. "Independent contractors" generally do not fall within the definition of an "employee" unless statute requires their classification as an employee; or when the individual is titled an independent contractor for tax purposes but is actually an employee under workers' compensation definitions.

Two disparate views of the difference between an "employee" and an "independent contractor" exist, one applied by the IRS and a broader view enforced by the insurance industry and industrial/labor commissions countrywide. Workers' compensation-defined "employees" encompass more than just hourly or salaried workers; they can include what some incorrectly deem to be independent contractors (paid without withholding — a 1099). Certain tests are applied to differentiate between a "legal" employee and a true independent contractor for workers' compensation purposes. "Test" questions include these.

- Does the employer/contracting party control the individual's ways and means (i.e., does the employer tell the contractor when to show up, how to do the job, and when to leave or is the contractor free to come and go as he or she pleases)?
- Are the tools and materials supplied by the employer/contracting party?

- Does the "independent contractor" work for anyone else or does he contract solely with the employer?
- Does the "independent contractor" carry his/her own insurance?

Generally, the level of control is the deciding factor when classifying a worker as an employee or an independent contractor. The higher the degree of control over the worker, the more likely he will be considered an employee rather than an independent contractor. If the employer: 1) sets the hours and methods of doing the job, 2) supplies the tools and materials and/or 3) is the sole source of income for the contractor, the higher the likelihood that the worker will be considered an employee not an independent contractor.

This is only a representative sample of the questions that may be applied in determining employee or independent contractor status, and not all the tests have to affirmatively indicate status as an employee, only a preponderance of evidence is required. Statutes step in at times and assign a worker "employee" status even when the person might qualify as a true independent contractor.

Likewise, general contractors may find themselves responsible for injury to *de jure* employees who work directly for an uninsured subcontractor. In most states, employees of uninsured subcontractors are statutorily defined as employees of the general contractor.

A more detailed description and definition of independent contractors is found in Chapter 8.

Legal Structure and Workers' Compensation

Neither sole proprietorships, partnerships, LLCs nor corporations define "employee" or calculate the number of employees using the same methods. Further, most states do not differentiate between a full-time or part-time employee. Legal structure and statute dictate who qualifies as an employee and, ultimately, the number of employees (for statutory counting purposes).

Sole Proprietorships and Partnerships

Sole proprietors and partners are most often exempted from the workers' compensation law and do not count toward the total number of employees. In jurisdictions subscribing to this statutory precept, a three-member partnership with one other worker has, by such statute, only one employee. States that exclude sole proprietors and partners from the definition of "employee" generally allow these individuals to subject themselves to the law and the benefits if desired.

There are a few states that do not exempt partners from the definition of "employee" requiring coverage unless a specific rejection notice is filed. There are even a few states that require sole proprietors to be classified as an employee if there are other employees on staff. The few states that define sole proprietors and partners to be employees generally allow these individual to exclude themselves from coverage.

Corporate Officers

Corporate officers, whether compensated or not, are commonly subject to the workers' compensation law and are included in the calculation of the total number of employees. Although most workers' compensation statutes allow these corporate officers to exclude themselves from the protection, they are still included in the total calculation of employees regardless of their coverage status. Some states apply variations to this rule for not-for-profit corporations.

A corporation with three officers and one employee has, by statue, four employees even if the officers exclude themselves by endorsement.

Limited Liability Companies

Limited liability companies (LLCs) are unique entities designed to combine some of the tax benefits of a partnership with some of the legal protections afforded corporations. Each jurisdiction dictates whether the members and managers of an LLC are treated as partners not subject to the workers' compensation statute or as corporate officers who are subject to the law. Members are simply the owners of the LLC and may or may not participate in the day-to-day management of the company. Members involved in the management maintain a dual role as members and managers. How each state views and treats LLC members and managers is found in Appendix B.

Natural vs. Legal Persons

Differences among legal structures determine who is considered the "employer" and ultimately who is an "employee." An employer is always a person, either a natural person or a legal person.

- **Natural person:** A flesh and blood human being. In workers' compensation the employer is a natural person(s) in sole proprietorships and partnerships. Managers and members of an LLC are viewed as natural persons in a majority of states making these natural persons the employers.

- **Legal person (a.k.a. juridical person):** A legal fiction, a "person" created by statute and born with the filing of articles of incorporation (or organization). These legal persons are given the right to own property, sue and be sued. Corporations are legal persons. Several states consider LLCs a legal person, making the managers and members employees.

"Employers" are not required to be covered by workers' compensation, but statute requires employers to provide workers' compensation benefits for their "employees." Thus, the sole proprietor as the "natural person" employer is excluded from the count; but the corporate officer is included as an employee because he/she works for the corporation – a "legal person."

See Appendix B for more information regarding employee counts and those workers that do not qualify as employees under the workers' compensation law of each state.

Chapter 8

The General Contractor's Responsibility
to Provide Protection

Sound risk management essentially requires general contractors to contractually mandate that workers' compensation coverage be in place anytime a subcontractor is hired. And subcontractors cannot hide behind statute in contract situations; workers' compensation coverage can be contractually required regardless of statutory provisions (contracts can be more stringent than state law but not less so (exculpatory)).

Forty-four states [1] and the District of Columbia statutorily regulate workers' compensation benefits within the general contractor-subcontractor relationship. "Employees" (as defined earlier) of a subcontractor in these states must be provided workers' compensation benefits if an injury occurs. Benefits will be paid either by the injured employee's direct employer (the subcontractor) or by the general contractor who hired the subcontractor. The general contractor is statutorily assigned the responsibility of providing workers' compensation benefits to the uninsured subcontractor's injured employee, regardless of the number of employees working for the subcontractor. Plus, any additional premium for these *de jure* employees will be charged to the general contractor, even if no loss occurs.

A general contractor-subcontractor relationship should not be confused with the relationship between a principal/owner and an independent contractor.

- An "**independent contractor**" is an entity with whom a principal/owner directly contracts to perform a certain task or tasks. Independent contractors are generally engaged to perform operations not within the usual trade or business of the principal and such tasks are contract specific. All work required of the contract is performed by the independent contractor and employees. Independent contractors are typically not considered employees of the principal.

- A "**general contractor**" is an entity with whom the principal/owner directly contracts to perform certain jobs. Some or all of the enumerated tasks are subsequently contracted to other entities (subcontractors) for performance. For general contractor relationships to exist there must be three parties: a principal, an independent contractor and a subcontractor hired by the independent contractor. Independent contractor status changes to general contractor when any part of the work is subcontracted to another entity.

Principals are not commonly held financially responsible for any injury to the independent contractor's employees or any employees of subcontractors hired by the independent contractor (making the independent contractor a general contractor). But, as stated above, the general contractor is financially responsible for any injuries to the employees of an uninsured subcontractor.

Principles and General Contractors

If neither the general contractor nor the subcontractor has workers' compensation coverage, the principal/owner could potentially be sued by an injured worker to recover any out-of-pocket expenses incurred (medical bills and lost wages). However, it is unlikely that the principal will be held financially responsible as the principal does not statutorily qualify as an employer or a general contractor. Although not held to "employer" status, the principal could be sued under other theories of liability such as negligent supervision, failure to provide a safe work environment or any other negligence theories often ascribed to property owners. If sued, the principal's general liability policy or the workers' compensation policy (if one exists) should provide defense and payment if found liable.

Principals and general contractors should contractually require that any entity with which they contract provide workers' compensation insurance. The mere act of purchasing coverage works to prove that the independent contractor or any subcontractor does not believe an employee-employer relationship exists or is created.

Any contract between the principal and general contractor should specifically place the responsibility of confirming subcontractor workers' compensation coverage solely on the general contractor. The general contractor should agree via the contract that if it does not require and confirm the presence of such insurance, it could be held statutorily responsible for injury to any of the subcontractor's employees. Lastly, the general contractor must also agree to defend and hold the principal harmless in case of injury to any direct or *de jure* employee.

Creating a Subcontractor Relationship

General contractor-subcontractor relationships are not confined to the construction industry; the relationship is just more statutorily regulated in the construction industry than most others. General contractor-subcontractor relationships are created every day in other industries. A city hires a consultant to study traffic patterns; the consultant hires an engineering firm to do on-site studies creating a general contractor relationship. A corporation hires a business consultant who subcontracts the cost control management work to another party, also creating a general contractor relationship. General contractor-subcontractor relationships are created by an endless array of activities.

Workers' compensation laws regarding general contractor-subcontractor relationships are designed to create a safety net for any injured worker — assuring benefits will be paid by somebody. To avoid being held financially responsible for another entity's employees, the general contractor is prudent to contractually require any lower tier contractor to carry workers' compensation coverage.

Contractual risk transfer is detailed in Chapter 9.

---

[1] Alabama, Alaska, Arizona, Arkansas, Colorado, Connecticut, Florida, Georgia, Hawaii, Idaho, Illinois, Indiana, Kansas, Kentucky, Louisiana, Maryland, Massachusetts, Michigan, Minnesota, Mississippi, Missouri, Montana, Nebraska, Nevada, New Hampshire, New Jersey, New Mexico, New York, North Carolina, North Dakota, Ohio, Oklahoma, Oregon, Pennsylvania, South Carolina, South Dakota, Tennessee, Utah, Vermont, Virginia, West Virginia, Wisconsin, Wyoming.

Chapter 9
Contractual Risk Transfer and Workers' Compensation

Beyond contractually requiring "lower tier" contractors to maintain workers' compensation coverage, "upper tier" contractors should consider incorporating other requirements into their contracts and agreements.

- **"Upper tier"** refers to the principal (owner) and primary general contractor.
- **"Lower tier"** contractors are the subcontractors and sub-subcontractors.

Previous chapters have focused on the definition of an employee, who is considered an employer and who could be held financially responsible for an injury. But insurance is not the only risk transfer mechanism available to protect upper tier contractors from the financial impact of an injury to a worker who is not a direct employee. Contractual risk transfer's contribution to upper tier contractor protection is the focus of this chapter.

Basics of Contractual Risk Transfer

Effective contractual risk transfer requires specific transfer wording in the contract between the upper tier and lower tier contractors. Since these disparate financing and control techniques (insurance and contractual risk transfer) are ultimately intertwined, understanding how workers' compensation policies and insurers respond to contractual risk transfer language is paramount.

Commonly known as the "indemnification agreement," all contracts between upper and lower tier contractors should contain some form of indemnification and hold harmless wording. Provisions of such contractual wording may read as follows:

> *"For and in exchange for fair and equitable consideration, transferee (name of the lower tier contractor) agrees to indemnify, hold harmless and waive any right of subrogation against transferor (name of the upper tier contractor) from any and all loss or cost arising from bodily injury to (transferee's) employees, subcontractors or subcontractor's employees hired by (transferee)."*

This sample wording is limited to an upper tier contractor's exposure to injuries covered by workers' compensation. Broader wording can be used to cover other exposures such as bodily injury and property damage liability to third parties or liability arising out of completed operations.

Notice, there are three parties to contractual risk transfer: the transferor, the transferee and the financer. Each is defined as follows.

- **Transferors** – The party from which risk is being transferred. This may include the owner, the project management firm, and/or the general contractor. Other common terms for the transferor include indemnitee and promise.

- **Transferees** – The party accepting the risk. This can include the general contractor, subcontractors and sub-subcontractors. Other common terms include indemnitor and promisor.

- **Financer** – The party called on to respond financially. This can include the "transferee" or an insurance company.

Indemnification and hold harmless agreements are the essence of effective contractual risk transfer. Indemnification is the contractual obligation of one party (the indemnitor) to return another party (the indemnitee) to essentially the same financial condition enjoyed before the loss with no improvement or betterment. Hold harmless wording provides protection from the legal process and any accompanying liability and expense that may arise from an injury. Unlike contractual requirements to purchase workers' compensation, indemnification wording is not necessarily affected by, nor does it affect, the transferee's insurance coverage. It is purely a contractual issue requiring one party to stand in place of another.

There are three levels of contractual risk transfer commonly found in contracts.

- **Limited transfer:** The transferee accepts only the financial consequences of loss resulting from his sole negligence. If the transferor or another party contributes to the loss, the transferee is not financially responsible for that part of the loss. Essentially, the transferor is only protected for its vicarious liability arising out of the actions of the transferee. This level is allowed in every state.

- **Intermediate transfer**: The transferee agrees to accept the financial consequences of occurrences caused in whole or in part by its negligence. This includes if the transferor or another entity contributes to the loss in some way. Only a few states allow this degree of transfer.

- **Broad transfer**: Provides the greatest scope and requires the transferee to indemnify and hold harmless the transferor from all liability arising out of an incident, even if the act is committed solely by the transferor. This may qualify as an exculpatory contract and is illegal in most jurisdictions because the wording is considered "unconscionable." Unconscionable is defined as a contract that is unreasonable due to the unequal bargaining strength of the parties, or the result of undue influence or unfair tactics.

Regardless of which level of transfer is desired, consult with legal counsel familiar with the jurisdiction as any decision may be affected by statute. Individual states may allow nothing more than limited transfer contracts, where others may allow broad transfer.

Contractual Risk Transfer Done Right with Wrong Results

Contractual risk transfer's importance cannot be underestimated; nor should its effectiveness be overestimated. Recounting a recent claim will work to explain the dichotomy of this statement.

Three parties were involved in this suit – the general contractor, the subcontractor and a sub-subcontractor. The general contractor bid out all the work on a large commercial building project in a monopolistic state, awarding the contract to supply the structural steel and erection to the subject subcontractor. The subcontractor only supplied the structural steel and delivered it to the construction site; choosing to subcontract the erection work to a third party, the sub-subcontractor (allowable by contract).

The subcontractor was required to contractually agree to indemnify and hold the general contractor harmless for any bodily injury or property damage resulting solely from the acts of the subcontractor or contributed to by the subcontractor (an intermediate transfer). In like manner, the subcontractor required the sub-subcontractor to sign a contract containing the same risk transfer wording.

An employee of the sub-subcontractor fell and was injured. The injured worker sued the general contractor for gross negligence and reckless disregard for safety. The general contractor transferred the claim to the subcontractor to defend and indemnify, as was required by contract. Since the subcontractor contractually transferred its risk down to the sub-subcontractor, the direct employer of the injured worker was pulled into the suit and responsible to indemnify and hold the subcontractor harmless, and the subcontractor, the general contractor.

Had the general contractor not contractually required the subcontractor to indemnify and hold it harmless, it would have been wholly responsible for its own defense and ultimate payout. Likewise, had the subcontractor not transferred its exposure to the sub-subcontractor, it may have become the sole party responsible to pay any injury or damages. This is the main goal of contractual risk transfer, to make the entity closest to the activity (and thus with the most control over the situation) financially responsible for any injury that occurs.

So far the contractual risk transfer is operating as anticipated and planned, but additional facts must be known before the unveiling of the end of the story and the ultimate subjugation of the contractual risk transfer provisions.

The injured employee of the sub-subcontractor was tacking down a roof at a height of about three stories, walking backwards; he physically lifted up the safety barriers to get outside of them so he could complete the job. Continuing to tack while walking backwards he fell and was paralyzed. Illegal drugs were found in his system after required testing.

The subcontractor delivered the material, left the job site, and never returned for any reason. The subcontractor was not charged with the supervision of the job and was not even on site in the days leading up to or on the day of the injury.

Contractual risk transfer had done its job by placing the burden on the party closest to and best able to control the work methods and means, the sub-subcontractor. However, this is not how it ended. The case never made it to trial; it was settled by the insurance carriers involved. The sub-subcontractor paid $2 million, the subcontractor (who was not even there) paid $1 million and the general contractor got out paying only $200,000.

Had this case gone to trial and had the contractual provisions held up under state law the entire burden would likely have been borne by the sub-subcontractor. The general contractor may have had to ante-up if it were proven he failed to maintain a safe work environment (a requirement that cannot be transferred away); but the subcontractor would likely not have had to pay anything. If laws were upheld, the employee should have received nothing for violating safety rules and regulations and testing positive for drugs. But this is pure theory and conjecture since no court ever heard the case.

Waiver of Subrogation

Construction contracts of recent years have tried to require that lower tier contractors endorse a "waiver of subrogation" onto a workers' compensation policy in favor of the upper tier contractors. Many insurers have historically refused this request for reasons outside the scope of this chapter (although this trend is changing in some states). Waiver of subrogation endorsements should not be necessary if the contract between the parties already waives such rights.

Subrogation rights flow from the harmed party's right to be made whole by the party responsible for the loss. If the right to subrogate against the upper tier contractor is waived by contract prior to an injury, the insurer of the injured worker's employer (the transferee) has no right to subrogate either. Waiver of subrogation should be a part of the indemnification and hold harmless section of the contract, not provided by an endorsement to the policy.

If a particular state's statute affects the level of indemnification allowed, waiver of subrogation wording may need to be addressed in a separate paragraph within the contract to lessen the chance that the provision will be voided if the level of transfer is outside of allowable transfer provisions.

Conclusion

If a worker is injured, he or she likely will sue everyone within reach. This cannot be avoided. The goal of contractually required insurance, and the use of contractual risk transfer, is simply to place the ultimate financial burden on the party most directly related to and responsible for the injured party.

Chapter 10

Employees Exempt from Workers' Compensation

Employee-employer relationships regarding workers' compensation are complicated by the IRS, industrial commissions, the courts and state statute. Each has its own definition or applies a different test to define "employee."

Prior chapters discussed the difference between an independent contractor and an employee; the responsibility placed on upper tier contractors when lower tier contractors do not provide workers' compensation benefits for their direct employees; and the importance of contracts and contractual risk transfer in managing some of these relationships. This chapter will re-cap some previously covered information and apply it to "employment situations" exempt from statutory workers' compensation protection.

Who Is an Employee and How Many Are Required?

Thirty-six states and the District of Columbia require every employer with one employee or more to provide workers' compensation coverage. Only 14 states allow employers to forego coverage until they surpass a certain threshold number of employees; once eclipsed, it becomes necessary for employers in those states to provide benefits. A few of the "threshold" states lower the threshold number if the employer falls within a contractor classification.

"Employee" and "employer" were defined in Chapter 7. Remember, as a general rule, the "employer" is not required to be protected by workers' compensation, but "employees" must be protected as per individual state statutes. The determination often revolves around the entity's legal structure.

- **Sole Proprietorships:** A sole proprietor (individual owner) is the employer. The individual owner, in nearly every state, does not count towards the number of employees. A sole proprietor with no employees is not required to carry workers' compensation. Any employees other than the individual owner, whether full or part time, change this requirement. Generally, even when a sole proprietor is required to protect his employees, the individual owner is only protected if coverage is specifically elected; and not every state allows the proprietor the option of coverage. A few states extend coverage to the sole proprietor but allow the individual to exclude himself from coverage by filing a rejection form.

- **Partnerships:** Partners, like sole proprietors, are the employer and as such do not count towards the number of employees. While this is not true in every state, the majority treat partners and sole proprietors the same regarding calculation and the option to elect (and in a few states, reject) coverage.

- **Corporations:** Corporations are "legal persons" (defined in Chapter 7) and are considered the employer. The corporation itself does not qualify for workers' compensation coverage since it is, in reality, a fictitious person and the employer. Corporate officers are considered "employees" of this fictitious person and count towards the total number of employees. Most states allow certain corporate officers to exclude themselves from workers' compensation protection simply by completing a rejection form. Some states limit the number or position titles of officers who can be excluded. Not-for-profit corporations are viewed differently in a few states in that the corporate officers (usually volunteers) are not included as employees and do not count towards the total number of employees.

- **Limited Liability Company:** Limited Liability Companies (LLCs) are subject to a wider range of views regarding the inclusion or exclusion of the owners than are the previously defined entity types. Twenty-three states treat members and managers as the "employers," specifically excluding them from the employee count and coverage; 20 states view the LLC as the "employer" and treat members and managers as corporate officers and thus employees. Seven states and the District of Columbia combine these extremes by classifying the members and managers as "employees" or "employers" based on specific criteria such as: how the entity chooses to be taxed, the number of members/managers, the operation classification (managers or members included as an employee if construction class or "high hazard class," excluded otherwise), or the percentage of ownership.

- **Professional Associations:** Professional associations (PAs) as a business entity are limited to a few professions such as physicians, dentists, attorneys, architects and other like professionals. States' views of professional associations are more diverse than the disparity over LLCs. Many states treat PAs like corporations, making the organizers corporate officers and thus employees. Other states equate these entities to LLCs; still other states place these entities in a separate class. Adding to the confusion, different insurance carriers in the same state might view PAs differently; one might consider them like partnerships while another carrier might treat them like corporations.

  Professional Associations are more like corporations from a legal standpoint than any of the other business types presented. The existence rights and provisions of a PA may not be the same in every state, but there are similarities.

- Professional Associations like corporations are created by the filing of Articles of Incorporation.
- Professional Associations and corporations can exist apart from the individuals that formed them (they exist

as a legal person), meaning the PA can own property, sue, be sued and incur debt and they can live beyond the natural life of the founders.

- Both Professional Associations and corporations can sell stock.

  Individual state statutes must be consulted to decide if professional association organizers are considered "employees" or "employers." If there is a disagreement among insurers, legal assistance may be required, or the respective department of insurance may need to be consulted

Worker's compensation protection is not required when the number of employees falls below the requisite number. Knowing the threshold and the definition of an employee in a particular state is paramount when placing workers' compensation for multi-state clients. As mentioned above, only 13 states allow a threshold greater than one "employee."

Employments Not Subject to Workers' Compensation

Certain "employment" situations and arrangements are exempt from the requirements of workers' compensation. Each state views exempted employment classes differently. Some allow total exclusion, while others may require coverage if certain thresholds are breached (generally very high thresholds in comparison to the standard requirements).

Casual Labor – No Workers' Compensation Required

Workers engaged in casual labor on behalf of the employer are not considered "employees" and are not required to be protected by a workers' compensation policy. This exclusionary provision applies in nearly every state with each applying different requirements to the exception.

- States may simply define casual labor and exclude the requirement to provide protection. Some states apply subjective terms to this definition such as "brief," "occasional," "irregular," "sporadic" or "infrequent," which may require arbitration or litigation to objectify.
- States may assign a maximum dollar limit that can be paid or a maximum number of days the job can last before the work is no longer considered "casual."
- States may assign a number of "casual employees" allowed.

Casual labor is generally defined as work that is not in the usual course of trade, business, occupation or profession of the employer (contracting party). This could include relationships such as a manufacturer hiring a landscaping company to maintain the grounds; or the owner of an insurance agency hiring a carpenter to upgrade the office. The contractors hired are not performing duties that would normally be done by any employee; they are doing work outside the normal operational requirements. Essentially, a casual laborer is one that does not directly promote or advance the employer's business or operation.

Other Employments Often Exempt from Workers' Compensation

Having fewer than the requisite number of employees and casual labor "employees" are just two of the employment situations that are exempt from workers' compensation statutes. Other employment relationships not subject to workers' compensation protection requirements include the following.

Domestic employees: Most states specifically remove the requirement of providing workers' compensation protection for domestic employees. Some states place a payroll limit or a numerical limit above which coverage is once again required.

Agricultural, Farm, Ranch, Aquaculture employees: Nearly every state excludes these workers from the definition of an "employee" and do not require coverage be provided to these workers. Like domestic employees, some states do limit the exception to operations or individuals with less than a specified number of workers or a specified payroll amount. A few states limit this exception with special provisions such as the type of work being performed or the familial relationships.

Commissioned Real Estate Agents: Many states remove the requirement to provide workers' compensation protection to real estate agents or subagents paid purely on a commission basis. This exclusion does not apply in every state.

The above are the most commonly found exclusions to the workers' compensation requirement, but there are several

84

beyond these that may only apply in a few states. This is not an all-inclusive list.

- Volunteer ski patrol employees
- Members of the clergy
- Some taxicab drivers
- Professional athletes
- Athletic contest officials
- Officers of non-profit associations and corporations
- Direct sale people (i.e. Mary Kay consultants and directors)
- Newspaper re-sellers
- Musicians/performers

Legal Recourse

If an exempted worker/employee is injured, the only recourse available to recover any medical costs or lost wages from the employer is the legal system. Essentially, the injured party has the same legal rights as a member of the general public, but the injured party also has to prove that the employer was negligent in causing the injury or illness. The employer is allowed the same defenses as were available prior to the enactment of workers' compensation laws.

- ***Assumption of Risk:*** Proving negligence requires evidence that a duty of care is owed. When an employee assumes the risk of an inherently dangerous or recognizably dangerous activity, the duty of care is lifted from the employer. With no required duty of care, there can be no negligence. Employees in hazardous occupations are believed to understand the hazards and to assume the risk of injury.

- ***Contributory or Comparative Negligence*** (depending on the state): This doctrine of defense states that if the injured person was even partially culpable in causing or aggravating his own injury, he is barred or severely limited in the amount of recovery from the other party.

- ***Fellow Servant Rule:*** Defense against employer negligence asserting that an employee's/worker's injury was caused by a fellow employee not by the acts of the employer. If proven, negligence is not chargeable against the employer and recovery could be severely limited or barred.

Unless negligence can be proven, no finding of guilt or a requirement to pay will materialize.

Workers' Compensation Coverage Provided

Workers' compensation coverage can be extended to many of these exempt employments by attaching one of the available Voluntary Compensation Endorsements. These endorsements extend workers' compensation protection to employments customarily exempted by individual state law by allowing the employer to designate the class of employees they wish protected. Essentially, workers become de facto employees, removing their need to sue and prove negligence and the employer's requirement to pay for and provide a defense.

See Appendix B for more information on exempt employees. Appendix D lists and describes most available workers' compensation endorsements.

Chapter 11

Extraterritorial Considerations – When to Add a '3.A.' State

Out-of-state and other state jurisdiction problems arise at the junction of two concepts: 1) Extraterritoriality and 2) Reciprocity. Extraterritoriality deals with employees who leave a state and reciprocity relates to how the state deals with employees entering the state.

- *Extraterritoriality:* How does the state's workers' compensation policy respond when one or several workers leave the state or states providing coverage to perform operations for or conduct duties on behalf of and for the furtherance of the employer's business? Does the workers' compensation coverage extend to that state?

- *Reciprocity:* How does the state to which the worker has travelled for work view the workers' compensation coverage carried by the employer in the "sending" state? Does the receiving state's workers' compensation law apply to the employer sending the workers? Does the sending employer's workers' compensation policy satisfy the receiving state's workers' compensation statutes?

Knowing where employees regularly work, and might temporarily work, during the policy period is absolutely essential when planning workers' compensation protection. Potential coverage gaps or the complete loss of protection are possible when employees conduct operations on behalf of the employer in states where the insured does not have a business location (an office address). These extraterritorial exposures must be discovered, planned for and managed in the policy.

Two methods/options are offered by the workers' compensation policy to manage the exposure created when employees are injured working in jurisdictions other than the employer's domicile state or a branch-location state. Workers' compensation extends protection and benefits to states listed as either "Primary/ 3.A." states or an "Other State" also known as a "3.C." state.

Deciding which category, 3.A. or 3.C., to place a particular state is not always crystal clear. A haze often surrounds workers in other states or the staffing of employees from another state. All jurisdictions except Connecticut and New Jersey have specific statutes addressing an employer's extraterritorial exposures. The following paragraphs attempt to clarify a few of the complex problems surrounding extraterritorial coverage decisions. Variability of state laws does not allow state-specific information to be presented.

Primary States (3.A.) Listing Requirements

State of domicile and branch office states should obviously be scheduled as 3.A. states. Employers whose employees work exclusively from fixed locations in the domiciled state or a listed branch location have little or no concern over extra jurisdictional exposures. The jurisdictional choices are rather straightforward unless one of the branch states is a monopolistic fund state.

Monopolistic states require the insured to purchase a workers' compensation policy from the state. Only four monopolistic states are still in operation: North Dakota, Ohio, Washington and Wyoming. Insureds operating in one of these states must purchase the workers' compensation protection from the state but will require an alternate means to secure employers' liability coverage. This will be discussed in a later chapter.

Extraterritorial coverage dilemmas arise when employees travel and work outside the scheduled "3.A." domicile and/or branch office states. All the information surrounding the employment situation in question must be known in order to be able to pinpoint which states necessitate scheduling as a primary 3.A. jurisdiction. Most likely, there is no specific guidance offered by the applicable state's statute nor will the underwriters be able or willing to provide a definitive answer regarding a particular state's need to garner status as a primary coverage state. Often the court will be the final word in a question of jurisdiction. When the court gets involved, the outcome is seldom beneficial to the agent that placed the coverage. Making the determination before the injury and erring on the side of caution is preferable. Reaching a conclusion is made easier when the exposure is realized, and the necessary information is available.

Employee Options

Employees injured in the course of employment for either a direct employer or a de jure employer (an employer created by law as detailed in previous chapters) potentially have several options regarding which state's workers' compensation benefits they are allowed to claim. They can choose the greater of these.

- Benefits available from their state of residence.
- Benefits extended from the state in which they primarily work.
- Benefits available in the state in which the injury occurred.
- Benefits prescribed by the state in which the employer's workers' compensation coverage is provided.

However, statutes or the common law in each state serve to greatly limit these options. State industrial commissions and/or the courts have developed specific tests to judge from which jurisdiction an injured worker can demand or expect benefits. Statutory and common law tests are either significant contact based, or contract of hire based.

Jurisdictional Tests

"Significant contact" tests base jurisdictional decisions around the employee. Three primary tests/questions work to determine which states need to be scheduled as primary, 3.A. states.

- Where does the employee live?
- Where does the employee primarily work?
- In what state was the contract of hire made?

If a "preponderance of contact" evidences a state not listed as a 3.A. state, there may be a gap in protection. For example, the employer, ABC Plumbers, located in State "A," hires James who lives just across the state line in State "B." James goes into State "A" every morning to pick up his job orders and once a week to get his paycheck, but nearly all of his jobs are near his home in State "B." ABC does not have a business office location in State "B." Should State "B" be listed as a 3.A. state?

Evidence indicates that State "B" has significant contact with the employee and thus should be listed as a primary state. Since the bulk of the employee's work is in State "B," it is likely that the injury will occur there. Further, State "A's" law may allow, or the courts may decide, that the employee is eligible for the higher benefits offered by State "B" as per the employee options listed above.

Even in states that do not apply the "significant contact" assessment, agents may be well-served to apply this three-question test when deciding which states to list as primary coverage states. Since civil trials are decided based on a "preponderance of evidence," using this test may prove conservatively cautious, but accurate.

"Contract of hire" states approach the issue of extraterritorial jurisdiction from the employment contract standpoint. The state of hire is essentially the deciding factor. The vast majority of states statutorily subscribe to this approach. However, court decisions often hearken back to the "significant contact" test.

Four tests apply in contract of hire jurisdictions to decipher whether another state is required to be listed as a 3.A. state. Not every "contract of hire" state utilizes the same qualifiers, but the majority extend benefits to employees meeting any of the following requirements.

- Is the employment principally localized in this state?
- Is the employee working under a contract of hire made in this state for employment not principally localized in any state?
- Is the employee working under a contract of hire made in this state for employment principally localized in another state whose worker's compensation law is not applicable to the employer?
- Is the employee working under a contract of hire made in this state for employment outside the United States?

If any of the tests are satisfied, employees working in other states are extended the benefits they would receive just as if they were working in the subject state. This is conditioned on, as detailed in upcoming paragraphs, the laws of the states in which the employee is working, specifically the reciprocity provisions.

Illinois is a contract of hire state. In 2006, its Supreme Court rendered a decision in <u>Mahoney v. Industrial Commission</u> that may have stepped beyond the bounds of "reasonable" interpretation of the contact of hire provisions when the court proclaimed, "the Act 'clearly states that site of the contract for hire is the exclusive test for determining the applicability of the Act to persons whose employment is outside Illinois where the contract of hire is made within Illinois'."

Mahoney began work for United Airlines' Chicago, Ill., terminal in 1969; working there until 1993. He voluntarily transferred to Orlando, Fla., in 1993. After moving to Florida, Mahoney purchased a house, remarried and only returned to Illinois for occasional training or to visit relatives; evidentiary proof he fully established residence in Florida.

He suffered compensable injuries in 1999 and 2001, both while working at the Florida location. At the time of his first injury he had been a Florida resident for nearly six years.

Mahoney received the requisite benefits allowed/required under the Florida Workers' Compensation Act, but he subsequently filed claim under the Illinois Workers' Compensation act asserting that the "contract of hire" provisions entitled him to Illinois benefits, which are somewhat higher than Florida's. The Illinois Supreme Court agreed and awarded him benefits under Illinois law.

Another State's Laws – Reciprocity

Not every state will recognize another state's extraterritorial provision. Essentially, some states don't care what another state law provides; employees working in their jurisdiction will abide by, and be subject to, the law of the state in which the employee is working, allowing the employee more benefit selection options.

The third "contract of hire" test, "Is the employee working under a contract of hire made in this state for employment principally localized in another state whose worker's compensation law is not applicable to the employer?" highlights this non-reciprocity opinion and requires knowledge of the law of any state where employees are working, whether temporarily or principally. If the employee is working in a reciprocal state, the domicile state benefits will apply; employees injured in a non-reciprocal state may subject the employer to a gap in coverage as the employee may be allowed to choose the other state's benefits. Employers, and their agents, with employees working principally in another state should not depend on this extraterritorial extension of coverage to provide the necessary workers' compensation benefits.

Knowing reciprocal status between states will allow better decisions when considering the need to extend primary 3.A. status to a particular state. Difficulty lies in the fact that the states do not have relatable reciprocal agreements. For instance, Oregon fully reciprocates with 22 states, according to the state Web site, while Idaho only lists seven states with which it reciprocates.

Each state develops its own reciprocal agreements. States that mutually honor others' extraterritorial provisions limit the injured employee's choice of jurisdictional benefits to those of the home state or state to which the employee is primarily assigned. Employees injured while working in a non-reciprocating state may have their choice of any of the four employee options previously discussed; and a court will likely participate in this determination.

Several states offer limited reciprocity, even to states with which they freely reciprocate otherwise. Limited reciprocation may be based on the employer's business classification, the amount of time the employees are in the state or the number of employees working in the state. If these thresholds are eclipsed, coverage must be extended to that state via a 3.A. listing.

Florida, Montana, Nevada, New York, Washington (a monopolistic state) and possibly Illinois will not honor another state's extraterritorial provisions when the employer is in the construction industry. When a contractor's employees are working, even temporarily, in one of these states, the state must be listed as a 3.A. state. Massachusetts is required to be listed as a 3.A. state anytime an employee is working there, regardless of the classification of the employer. Payroll earned in these states must be calculated using the respective state's rates.

New Mexico and Wisconsin both restrict reciprocity and mandate 3.A. status for any employer having three or more employees in their respective states, even on a temporary basis. South Carolina extends the employee count to four or more. Alabama, Arkansas and North Dakota (a monopolistic state) are the other examples of states applying limited extraterritorial reciprocity.

Assigning Primary / 3.A. Status

No fixed rules or guidelines exist to delineate exactly the circumstances under which a particular state should be assigned 3.A. status. Lawyers are even unwilling to pin themselves down to a "yes" or "no," only an "it depends." Following are recommendations to consider when determining whether a state should be scheduled as a 3.A. state. Without specific information regarding a particular employment situation, these are not "rules," only suggestions. These states that may require assignment to 3.A. status.

- The employer's state of domicile – the "home office" (without question).
- The employer's state of incorporation if the employer incorporated in a state other than where the primary operations are carried out (the home office). Employers sometimes incorporate in states other than where they operate for tax governance reasons; the state of incorporation may need to be listed as a 3.A. state.
- States where branch offices are located.

- Any state outside office-location states where the employer hires temporary "employees" solely to perform operations in that state of hire.
- Any state where a subcontractor is hired to perform work on behalf of a general contractor if proof of workers' compensation is not provided. Remember, general contractor-subcontractor relationships are not limited to construction operations. Uninsured subcontractors may become de jure employees in the other state based on that state's law.
- Any state that has "significant contact" with an employee. If the employee lives and primarily works in a state different than the employer, that state should be assigned status as a 3.A. state.
- Any state where employees work more than a prescribed number of days during the policy year. Ninety days may be a good gauge, but this is not a concrete number. Individual state law should be reviewed for jurisdictional requirements.
- Any state that does not reciprocate with the employer's state of domicile or scheduled branch locations.
- States with limited reciprocity provisions.
- The state in which the "contract of hire" was executed (even if the employee moves).
- Any state where the employee works on a regular basis (60 to 75 percent of the time might be a good guide).
- Any state where the employer has more than a pre-determined number of employees working for longer

than a few consecutive days. Three or more employees longer than 30 days may be a good measure.

- Monopolistic states require a separate policy.

Remember, these are merely recommendations and not rules to be followed in every case. Additionally, underwriters may be unwilling to extend 3.A. status even when a good case can be made for the need.

Not every state in which employees are working will require or even be eligible by underwriting guidelines for assignment as a 3.A. state; but there still exists the potential for an injury in another state to trigger that state's workers' compensation law. The second option offered in the workers' compensation policy for extending coverage to extraterritorial jurisdictions is the Other States provision. These are the 3.C. states.

Other States Insurance (3.C.)

Part Three – "Other States Insurance" is essentially two paragraphs within the entire workers' compensation policy, but the coverage extended, and the potential problems created by noncompliance with this small section must not be overlooked or underestimated. The other states section dictates how the workers' compensation policy will respond if and when an employee is injured in a non-3.A. state but due to extraterritorial reciprocity problems is given the option to choose the benefits mandated by the state of injury rather than the state of domicile.

Other states (3.C.) coverage allows the employer's workers' compensation policy benefits to comply with the statutory benefits required by the state where an employee is injured but in which the insured: 1.) does not currently have on-going operations, and 2.) does not plan to have on-going operations during the policy period such as would necessitate its scheduling as a primary coverage state. Employees injured while working in a scheduled 3.C. state will receive the benefits prescribed under that state's law if made necessary by application of law or a court decision. Effectively the workers' compensation policy responds and pays benefits in listed 3.C. states just as if the state was scheduled under 3.A.

It is absolutely essential that any state qualifying for 3.A. status based on the assignment tests detailed previously be extending 3.C. status when the underwriter, for whatever reason, is unwilling to assign 3.A. status to that state. Employees are obviously working in or have significant contact with those states and a court may decide that the injured employee is eligible for the state-of-injury benefits rather than those mandated in the state of domicile or coverage.

From an errors and omissions (E&O) perspective, documenting that 3.A. status was requested but was disallowed by the underwriter is imperative. Get the denial in writing, signed by the underwriter and keep it in the insured's file. This will serve as a defense and hopefully help to avoid any gaps in the desired protection. (It will also serve as a good reminder at renewal to follow up to find out if status in that state has changed, necessitating 3.A. status.) Once the underwriter officially denies 3.A. status, specifically list that state in the 3.C. section of the application and confirm that the state is present on the declarations page when the policy arrives.

Employers should structure their "other states" protection to include any state to which the underwriter is willing to extend coverage. Most E&O carriers recommend 3.C. status be garnered with the phrase, "All states other than 3.A. states and monopolistic states." If the underwriter is willing to provide such a broad 3.C. extension, so much the better for the client; however, some carriers will not allow this breadth of protection due either to license status (the carrier may only be licensed in a few states), or the desire for greater information regarding the location and activities of the employees.

At minimum, other states (3.C.) status should be extended to all of these.

- Bordering states. This negates the exposure arising from employees that live in one state but work in the primary state.
- Any state to which income taxes are paid or would be paid.
- States to which employees may travel to attend classes, conventions or other meetings.

Recommended – Preferred 3.C. Status Wording

To properly extend workers' compensation protection for other states, it may be advisable to trigger 3.C. status.

- Specifically scheduling those states that qualify for 3.A. status as per the assignment test delineated above but which the underwriter will not allow such assignment.
- Specifically listing the bordering states and the other states as recommended in the preceding paragraph.
- Completing the schedule of protection by adding the terminology, "All remaining states other than 3.A. states and monopolistic states."

Following the above advisory, the Other States (3.C.) blank for a North Carolina domiciled risk with employees occasionally working in surrounding states plus Maryland and New Jersey, and commonly attending seminars in Texas may be completed as follows:

"SC, GA, TN, VA, MD, NJ, TX and all remaining states other than 3.A. states and monopolistic states."

While this may seem rather long (yes, there is limited space, but the comments section can be used), it succeeds in assuring that states that need to be listed are listed. It also shows the client that the agency has gone above and beyond to manage his exposures.

Underwriting's Bogus Claim

"We can't list _____ as a 3.C. state because we are not licensed there." This is a bogus claim; underwriters may not want to list the state, but they can. Paragraph A.3. under Part Three – Other States Insurance says: "We will reimburse you (the named insured) for the benefits required by the workers' compensation law of that state if we are not permitted to pay the benefits directly to persons entitled to them."

Other than not being licensed in the state, why would the carrier not be allowed to pay the injured worker? Just because they don't want to list a state doesn't mean they can't.

Penalties for Non-Compliance

Penalties for not properly scheduling a state as a 3.A. or a 3.C. jurisdiction are clear and potentially severe, especially in a state that should be classified as a 3.A. state on the day the policy goes into effect.

NCCI's workers' compensation policy specifically declares: "If you have work on the effective date of this policy in any state not listed in Item 3.A. of the Information Page, coverage will not be afforded for that state unless we are notified within thirty days."

Any state required to be scheduled as a 3.A. state but not listed on the day the policy is effective or within 30 days of the effective date will not be afforded protection. If an injury occurs in an unlisted-but-should-be 3.A. state, all benefits required of that state will be paid strictly by the employer. Knowing up front which states are required to be scheduled as 3.A. states is essential in order to avoid this denial of coverage. This is why proper file documentation is imperative if the underwriter refuses to list a state as a primary 3.A. state. Listing it as a 3.C. state when the underwriter refuses to extend primary status may mitigate some of these exposures, but there is no guarantee.

Injuries occurring in a state not requiring 3.A. status but which is also not extended coverage under the other states, 3.C., provision will subject the insured to a potential gap in benefits but not a total denial of coverage. For example, an employer domiciled in State "C" has an employee injured in State "D." The breadth of operations in State "D" does not necessitate 3.A. status but neither was the policy adequately planned to extend "Other States" (3.C.) status to "D." If the employee, via an industrial commission or court decision, qualifies to receive "D's" benefits, the employer's workers' compensation policy will only pay the benefits available in State "C." The difference between "C's" and "D's" benefits will be paid by the employer. Had State "D" been covered under the Other States, 3.C., provision, the employer's workers' compensation policy would have paid benefits as if State "D" were a primary, 3.A., state.

If the insured begins operations in a 3.C. state during the policy period, the insurance carrier is to be notified "at once." If notification does not meet policy requirements, any injury will be subject to the same denial of benefits found when a 3.A. listing is required but not made there will be no coverage.

Conclusion

Extraterritorial exposures and reciprocity problems open the employer and the agent to many pitfalls and potential coverage gaps. This is a complex subject that requires specific information regarding the states in which a particular employer works or might potentially work.

Chapter 12
The Surprising Importance of Employers' Liability Protection

Workers' compensation insurance was designed to be, and remains, the employee's sole remedy to recover medical costs and lost wages resulting from bodily injury suffered in the "course of employment" (as defined earlier). There are, however, bodily and financial injuries that: 1) fall outside workers' compensation protection, and 2) are excluded by the general liability policy.

Part Two – Employers' Liability Insurance dovetails to connect the workers' compensation policy and the commercial general liability policy, filling gaps created by the narrowness of the workers' compensation policy and exclusions in the commercial general liability policy.

Although included as part of the workers' compensation policy, employers' liability insurance is similar to, and contains components of, the commercial general liability and the workers' compensation policies. Part Two shares slightly more similarities with the commercial general liability policy than with workers' compensation (Part One).

Employers' Liability and Commercial General Liability

Employers' liability and commercial general liability coverage have some striking similarities.

- **They both require negligence be proven by the injured person or entity before any payment of benefits**. Workers' compensation is a "no-fault," exclusive remedy system where the only requirement to receive the statutorily prescribed benefits is an injury arising out of and in the course and scope of employment. Conversely, the employers' liability section (Part Two) requires the injured party (be they the employee, a family member or another entity) to prove that: 1) there was a duty owed to them, 2) the duty was breached by the insured, 3) an injury occurred and 4) the breach of duty was the proximate cause of the injury. If negligence cannot be proven, the insured has no legal liability and the insurer has no duty to indemnify the injured party.

- **They both apply a specific limit**. Limits in the workers' compensation policy are mandated by state statute, regardless of the amount. Employers' liability coverage has a specific limit of liability, except in one (NY) or possibly two states (MA) where the coverage is unlimited. Basic employers' liability limits are $100,000 per occurrence for bodily injury; $100,000 per employee for bodily injury by disease; and

$500,000 aggregate for bodily injury by disease. These limits can be increased by endorsement and the payment of additional premium.

- **Coverage is written on a per occurrence basis with an aggregate limit for injury by disease**. As above, the bodily injury limit is per occurrence with no aggregate; however, bodily injury by disease is subject to an annual aggregate limit.

- **Additional limits are available from an umbrella/excess policy**. Part One – Workers' compensation, as stated above, pays whatever is required by statute with only a statutory cap. Employers' liability (Part Two) is subject to the limits shown on the declarations page. If additional limits are desired, the underlying limits are adequate and the insurance company is willing to provide the additional protection, an umbrella or excess policy can sit over the employers' liability coverage to increase the available limits.

- **Defense is provided in excess of the coverage limits**.

Employers' Liability and Workers' Compensation

Employers' liability coverage dovetails and correlates with workers' compensation benefits.

- **Bodily injury or financial injury for which the insured is held legally liable must arise out of and in the course and scope of the employee's**

employment for the insured. Employers' liability coverage is payable only when an outside party suffers bodily injury or financial injury as a direct result of the work-related injury suffered by the employee. There is one extension of employers' liability coverage allowing the eligible "outside party" to be the employee. The breadth and provisions of coverage will be discussed in a later section.

- **The employment leading to injury must occur in or be attributable to a 3.A. listed (primary) state**. Subject to the extraterritorial jurisdiction requirements of each state and the additional considerations highlighted in a prior section of this chapter, this coverage part only extends protection if the employee is injured in a state or strictly eligible for benefits from a state specifically scheduled under 3.A. Employees injured while working in a non-3.A. state may not be eligible for extraterritorial extensions of coverage from the primary state of domicile due to lack of reciprocity between the subject states; if such reciprocity is unavailable, employers' liability coverage does not extend to any third party claims arising out of that injury.

- **Bodily injury must occur during the policy period and the last day of any exposure causing or aggravating a bodily injury by disease must occur during the policy period.** These same requirements apply before an injury can be compensable in the workers' compensation policy.

'Outside Party'

Before moving any further into the discussion of employers' liability protection, the term "outside party," used several times above and several more times in the remainder of the employers' liability discussion, must be understood as it relates to the workers' compensation policy and the commercial general liability policy. For this discussion, "outside party" has two definitions based on which coverage form is being discussed. This difference must be clearly evident before moving forward in this discussion.

Workers' compensation is a "three-known-party" policy: 1) the employer/insured, 2) the employee (the injured), and 3) the insurance carrier. All three are known from the beginning. Any individual or entity not qualifying as one of these known parties is considered an "outside party."

Commercial general liability coverage also involves three parties, but only two are known up front: 1) the insured (as defined in the policy); and 2) the insurer. The third party, the injured party is unknown making them the "outside party" in a commercial general liability policy.

Work Compensation and CGL Gaps Necessitate Employers' Liability Insurance

Why coverage as significant and crucial as employers' liability is routinely ignored is baffling. Employers' liability protection has been mistakenly viewed as a throw-away coverage that is simply tacked onto the workers' compensation policy. Understanding and focusing attention on workers' compensation and general liability is seen as a better use of the agent's time. One reason may be that few agents have ever been a part of an employers' liability claim.

But as mentioned earlier, the importance of this dovetail coverage cannot and should not be overlooked. This is the tie that binds two major coverages together. Such gap coverage deserves as deep an understanding as do the coverages it joins together.

Workers' Compensation and CGL Provisions

Part Two – Employers' Liability insurance fills the gaps between the workers' compensation policy and the commercial general liability policy. Workers' compensation coverage does not have any specific exclusions, per se. Penalties are assessed, but no specific exclusions apply. The limited breadth of protection necessitates this additional coverage. Conversely, the commercial general liability policy contains two specific employee injury exclusions that underlie the need for this dovetail protection.

Workers' compensation insurance benefits are statutorily mandated and restricted to costs directly assignable to a specific employee injured in the course and scope of employment. Coverage is not designed to compensate any outside party, only the injured employee or the employee's dependents if the worker dies as a result of the work related injury or illness (death benefits are considered payments directly attributable to and solely for the "benefit" of the deceased employee not for the injury suffered by any outside party).

Commercial general liability is different. Two exclusions found in ISO's CGL policy preclude the extension of coverage to any party suffering bodily injury or financial loss as a result of an injury to an employee. These exclusions are:

- **Exclusion "d." Workers' Compensation and Similar Laws** excludes any obligation of the insured under a workers' compensation, disability benefits or unemployment compensation law or any similar law.

- **Exclusion "e." Employers' Liability** excludes bodily injury to: 1.) An employee of the insured arising out of and in the course of employment by the insured; or while performing duties related to the conduct of the insured's business; or 2.) The spouse, child, parent, brother or sister of that "employee" as a consequence of an employee injured in the course and scope of employment. Exclusion "e." applies whether the insured may be liable as an employer or in any other capacity and to any obligation to share damages with or repay someone else who must pay damages because of the injury. Exclusion "e." does not apply to liability assumed by the insured under an "insured contract."

Exclusion "e." is designed to exclude bodily injury arising out of and in the course and scope of employment to any person qualifying as an "employee" and not already excluded by the workers' compensation exclusion (exclusion "d."). This is the "catch-all" employee exclusion.

The limited provisions of the workers' compensation policy and the exclusions in the commercial general liability policy combine, with one exception, to preclude coverage for **any** injury or loss suffered by an outside party as a result of an injury to an employee. This gap is closed, to some extent, by the employers' liability insurance.

Before jumping into the coverage provided by the employers' liability policy, the exception to the commercial general liability policy's exclusion "e." requires exploration and comment.

Exception to the Employers' Liability Exclusion in the CGL

Liability to an "outside party" arising out of an injury to an employee is covered by the unendorsed commercial general liability policy, provided such liability is contractually assumed prior to the injury under an "insured contract" as defined in the applicable CGL form.

Go back and reread "Contractual Risk Transfer Done Right with Wrong Results" in chapter 9, which recounts an employee injury claim that accurately highlights how this exception to the commercial general liability's employers' liability exclusion (exclusion "e.") applies. Each higher tier contractor transferred its exposure down to the lower tier contractors beginning with the general contractor and ending at the sub-subcontractor.

Since the sub-subcontractor contractually agreed to assume the liability of the upper-tier contractor prior to the injury, the sub-subcontractor's general liability policy responded and paid for injury to the sub-subcontractor's own employee. So, yes, an insured's general liability policy may respond and pay for injury to its own employee when such employee contractually qualifies as an "outside party" (defined previously) by exception to the general liability policy exclusion.

Beware and do not depend on this automatic extension of coverage. Even though such is standard wording in ISO's CGL, many insurance carriers are removing this automatic protection by attaching the CG 21 39 exclusion to contractors (and many other classes of insureds) commercial general liability policies. The CG 21 39, titled "Contractual Liability Limitation," redefines an insured contract by removing definition "f." Removing "f." deletes coverage for the assumption of tort liability of another party via contract.

In short, the contractual risk transfer coverage as recounted above and detailed in earlier paragraphs will be negated in the CGL policy containing this exclusionary endorsement. Additionally, such contractual assumption is specifically excluded in the employers' liability coverage part. Attachment of this exclusion creates a large coverage gap in the contractual liability coverage available to the insured.

Many construction contracts request proof via the certificate of insurance that "broad form contractual liability" exists; this is a hold-over term from the years prior to the 1986

CGL revisions. However, stating that broad form contractual liability protection does in fact exist may actually be misrepresentation if the definition of "insured contract" has been limited by the attachment of the CG 21 39. Such misrepresentation may leave the client open to charges of breach of contract and the agent open to an errors and omissions suit. This is a wide gap!

Employers' Liability Coverages

Employers' liability policy wording specifies four types of claims to which this coverage part responds.

1. Third party-over actions
2. Loss of consortium (loss of family service)
3. Consequential bodily injury
4. Dual Capacity actions

Each of these is detailed in the following paragraphs.

Third Party-Over

While in college I spent one summer working for a manufacturing operation. There I learned a number of new skills and a lot about myself including why I was going to college. During my tenure I witnessed a workers' compensation claim in the form of a 15-year-old getting his hand caught in a large crimping machine next to my workstation (yes, there are a number of things wrong with the situation).

He developed a rhythm of putting in the blank, activating the machine and removing the completed piece. Finished parts were coming out very quickly; but somewhere along the way his timing was thrown off and he put the blank in at the precise moment he activated the machine (nope, no safety problems here).

Thousands of pounds of pressure per square inch landed on this kid's hand; but because the machine was unable to make a full resolution it did not release, trapping my co-worker's hand. The machine was not equipped with an emergency release mechanism and would not "let go."

This kid is screaming and crying (and I'm not ashamed to say I probably would have done the same, even as a 19-year-old). I'm standing there with no idea what to do. I don't want to pull him; the machine is far stronger than I and everyone else is frozen. Finally, my friend musters enough clarity to reach up and turn off the machine, at which point he is released. I catch him as he falls. He gets to his feet and takes off running with no clear destination. An older, more experienced worker grabs him and puts a tourniquet around his wrist to stop the bleeding.

At the end of this ordeal, a 15-year-old kid had two of his middle fingers removed because they were crushed beyond repair.

If there were sufficient grounds to prove negligence, he could have filed a products liability claim against the machine's manufacturer claiming, among other things, insufficient safety in the machine's design and lack of adequate guards.

A suit never materialized, but had it occurred, the equipment manufacturer would have discovered that the guards designed to protect the worker had been removed to speed up production (a fact I learned later). With this information, the manufacturer could have sued the employer for acting improperly.

This is an example of a third party-over suit where an employer is sued by an "other party" as a direct result of an injury to an employee. Any liability to the "other party" would be excluded from the workers' compensation coverage discussed previously; and coverage would also be excluded by the two commercial general liability policy exclusions.

Protection and payment can only be found in the employers' liability policy.

Loss of Consortium

Depending on the seriousness of the employee's injury, the family may suffer in ways that aren't compensated or even compensable by the workers' compensation coverage part. These include additional costs to hire outside help to provide the services that were provided by the injured employee, the loss of companionship (which does include sexual relations) and, in some jurisdictions, claims for emotional injury.

For example, additional expenses are incurred because a lawn service has to be hired to care for the injured employee's yard since he can no longer perform that task. A percentage of the lost wages are paid by the workers' compensation policy, but additional expenses are not necessarily contemplated by the workers' compensation policy and must be paid by the employers' liability section.

Consequential Bodily Injury

A work-related disease may be the best example of consequential bodily injury. If the employee were to contract a work-related infectious disease that was subsequently spread to another member of the immediate family, this would be a prime example of consequential bodily injury covered by the employers' liability policy.

To qualify for coverage, the consequential bodily injury must be the direct result of a work-related injury suffered by the employee.

Dual Capacity

Employers may have business-related contact with their employees outside the employee-employer relationship. These additional relationships can be in the form of a product supplier, service provider or as the owner of a premises. Such dual persona creating this increased contact may subject the employer to liability for injury to an employee that may occur at work, but which does not necessarily arise out of and in the course and scope of employment.

Dual persona relationships create employer obligations to the worker independent of those imposed on an insured strictly as the employer. In essence, the exclusivity of workers' compensation protection is waived in situations where the employer could be liable to the general public for the same injury.

My father worked as a plant electrician for a soft drink bottling company in the mid-1960s. As a "perk" the employees were allowed to take the ready-to-ship bottles directly off the line to drink while at work (they were ice cold and fresh, plus real sugar was still used back then).

Had my dad been poisoned by a contaminated drink ready for shipment to the general public, he, or his heirs, could have sued under the dual capacity doctrine to recover amounts outside the benefits payable under the workers' compensation coverage. In such an instance, the employer ceases being the employer and steps into a second role (a second persona) as a product supplier. The logic is, had this drink gone out to the general public, the supplier would have been faced with a products liability suit; and since the general public could have been exposed to the same injury, the injured employee can access the same redress for injuries suffered as any member of the general public.

Health care workers can also be subject to dual capacity relationships. Doctors and nurses injured in the course of employment may be cared for at the medical facility in which they work. Once the hospital or medical facility undertakes to provide care available to the general public, it has taken on a second persona (that of service provider) and potentially subjected themselves to the dual capacity doctrine.

Employers' Liability – Exclusions, Monopolistic States and Limits

The National Council on Compensation Insurance's (NCCI's) 1991 edition of the workers' compensation and employers' liability policy (see Appendix C) lists 12 specific exclusions applying to Section Two – Employers' Liability Insurance. Each of these exclusions is listed below and several are briefly explored in more detail.

- **Liability assumed under a contract**. As per earlier discussion, employers' liability for liability to an "outside party" assumed under contract is extended from the commercial general liability policy unless the definition of an "insured contract" has been altered by endorsement. If the CG 21 39 exclusionary endorsement has been attached, the employer's only source of protection is the workers' compensation policy (Part One) covering the medical costs and lost wages of the employee. Any "outside party" liability for an injury to an employee contractually transferred to the insured will have to be paid out of the insured employer's pocket.
- **Punitive or exemplary damages arising from an employee employed in violation of law**. Neither Part One – Workers' Compensation Insurance nor Part Two – Employers' Liability Insurance will cover the cost of any court-prescribed penalties or punishment arising out of an employee injured while illegally

employed. The workers' compensation coverage part has to pay normal benefits, just not additional benefits imposed by the courts.

- **Any bodily injury to an employee while knowingly employed by the insured in violation of the law**. Part One – Workers' compensation coverage will pay the statutorily required benefits (but no more) to any "employee" injured, even if such person is working in direct violation of the law with the full knowledge of the insured. However, the employers' liability part specifically excludes any coverage for illegal employees.

- **Any obligation imposed by a workers' compensation, occupational disease, unemployment compensation, or disability benefits law, or any similar law.** If the injury or loss is covered or supposed to be compensable under the workers' compensation policy, unemployment compensation policy or other such law it is not covered under employers' liability part.

- **Bodily injury intentionally caused or aggravated by the insured**. Covered, up to statutory limits, under the workers' compensation part but excluded in this coverage part.

- **Bodily injury occurring outside the United States of America, its territories or possessions, and Canada unless the injured employee is a citizen or resident of the United**

States of America or Canada who is temporarily outside these countries. Coverage is excluded for foreign nationals working outside of the coverage territory. Domestic employees working outside the coverage territory on a temporary basis are covered.

- **Damages arising out of coercion, criticism, demotion, evaluation, reassignment, discipline, defamation, harassment, humiliation, discrimination against or termination of any employee, or any personnel practices, policies, acts or omissions.** This is an Employment Practices Liability exposure covered under another policy type; besides, there is not necessarily any bodily injury arising out of these claims.

- **Bodily injury to any person in work subject to the Longshore and Harbor Workers' Compensation Act (33 USC Sections 901-950), the Non-appropriated Fund Instrumentalities Act (5 USC Sections 8171-8173), the Outer Continental Shelf Lands Act (43 USC Sections 1331-1356), the Defense Base Act (42 USC Sections 1651-1654), the Federal Coal Mine Health and Safety Act of 1969 (30 USC Sections 901-942), any other federal workers' or workmen's compensation law or other federal occupational disease law, or any amendments to these laws.** The policy can be endorsed as necessary to remove any or all five of these Federal

Compensation Act exclusions if such exposure exists. The available endorsements are:

- Longshoremen's and Harbor Workers' Compensation Act Coverage Endorsement – WC 00 01 06A
- Nonappropriated Fund Instrumentalities Act Coverage Endorsements – WC 00 01 08A
- Outer Continental Shelf Lands Act Coverage Endorsement – WC 00 01 09A
- Defense Base Act Coverage Endorsement – WC 00 01 01A
- Federal Code Mine Health and Safety Act Coverage Endorsement – WC 00 01 02
- **Bodily injury to any person subject to the Federal Employers' Liability Act (45 USC Sections 51-60), any other federal laws obligating an employer to pay damages to an employee due to bodily injury arising out of or in the course of employment, or any amendments to those laws.** The Federal Employers' Liability Act Coverage Endorsement (WC 00 01 04A) can be attached giving back employers' liability coverage for employees qualifying for protection under Federal liability laws.
- **Bodily injury to a master or a member of the crew of any vessel**. Two endorsements are available allowing the insured to provide coverage for employees subject to the provisions of maritime law.

- Maritime Coverage Endorsement (WC 00 02 01A) – This endorsement is used if the insured has no protection and indemnity (P&I) policy.
- Voluntary Compensation Maritime Coverage Endorsement (WC 00 02 03) – This endorsement is used to voluntarily extend coverage to employees not normally required to be protected by a workers' compensation policy.
- **Fines or penalties imposed for violation of federal or state law.** Neither the workers' compensation coverage part nor the employers' liability coverage section will pay any penalties assessed against the insured for violation of laws. Example violations include fines imposed by OSHA or other regulatory bodies for failure to provide a safe work environment or provide and/or require the use of personal protective equipment. These costs will be borne solely by the employer.
- **Damages payable under the Migrant and Seasonal Agricultural Worker Protection Act (29 USC Sections 1801-1872) and under any other federal law awarding damages for violation of those laws or regulations issued thereunder, and any amendments to those laws.** As above, there is no coverage for employment or employment conditions in violation of applicable laws.

The endorsements listed above will be detailed further in the upcoming paragraphs.

Monopolistic States

Only four monopolistic states remain in operation: North Dakota, Ohio, Washington and Wyoming. Insureds with on-going operations in one of these states must purchase workers' compensation protection from the state and must find an alternate means to secure employers' liability coverage.

Three methods are available to fill this protection gap to which employers operating in monopolistic states are subject.

1. **Stand-alone employers' liability coverage**. Employers domiciled and operating nearly exclusively in a monopolistic state can purchase a stand-alone employers' liability policy from a private insurer. These states do not offer this protection.

2. **Endorsement to the workers' compensation and employers' liability insurance policy**. WC 00 03 03C can be attached to an employer's policy operating in a non-monopolistic state with employees working in a monopolistic state and subject to that state's laws. The employer buys a separate workers' compensation policy from the state covering just the employees in the monopolistic state, and then they attach this endorsement to their domicile-state policy, listing the monopolistic states in which employees are involved in on-going operations.

3. **Endorsed onto the commercial general liability policy**. Employers domiciled in non-monopolistic states but with employees in monopolistic states may choose to endorse the commercial general liability policy to extend employers' liability benefits to cover the monopolistic state employees. As above, the workers' compensation policy is purchased from the state and the commercial general liability policy is endorsed to extend employers' liability protection. Each monopolistic state requires a state-specific endorsement. Some underwriters are unwilling to extend this protection via the CGL (especially if they are unwilling to allow the umbrella to sit over the employers' liability section).

Regardless of which method is chosen, extending employers' liability coverage to employees in monopolistic states is of utmost importance. As has been discussed in this chapter, employers' liability protection fills many gaps between the workers' compensation policy and the protection offered by the commercial general liability policy.

A Word about Limits

Standard limits offered by the employers' liability policy ($100,000 Each Occurrence for Bodily Injury, $100,000 Each Occurrence for Employee Disease with a $500,000 Employee Disease Aggregate) are just too low. Remember, this coverage serves to fill the gaps between the workers' compensation policy and the commercial general liability policy.

Workers' compensation coverage is limited only by statute and the commercial general liability protection is generally no less than $1 million per occurrence (sometimes higher); so why should the limits of the policy that fills this gap be so low?

Increasing employers' liability coverage limits is relatively inexpensive. Five hundred thousand dollar across the board limits ($500,000 / $500,000 / $500,000) increases the entire policy premium about 2 percent (this varies depending on the carrier), and jumping the coverage to $1 million / $1 million / $1 million increases the premium by only around 3 percent over standard. And anytime the umbrella carrier is willing to extend benefits over the employers' liability coverage that opportunity should be taken.

Employers' Liability Endorsements

Endorsements used to alter a few of the exclusions specific to employers' liability coverage were listed in earlier paragraphs. These endorsements are more specifically detailed below. Each alters to some extent both the workers' compensation (Part One) and employers' liability (Part Two) sections. A description of each endorsement, including the intent and eligibility factors, is presented, with each charted in Appendix D.

Longshoremen's and Harbor Workers' Compensation Act Coverage Endorsement (WC 00 01 06A)

Classifying a worker as a longshoreman or harbor worker requires the application of two specific tests: the "situs" and "status" tests. USL&HW benefits are extended to employees that meet both requirements.

- Situs requires that the employment be on, above or below navigable waters and adjoining areas. But working around or over water does not in itself qualify an individual for the benefits prescribed by the USL&HW Act. To qualify for such coverage requires satisfying the "status" test.

- Status as a longshoreman or harbor worker requires that the employment involve the loading and unloading of ships; or the maintenance, repair or dismantling of ships.

Unless both tests are satisfied, the employee is not a longshoreman or a harbor worker and is not eligible for the applicable benefits. An individual or group of employees working on a bridge above navigable waters does not necessarily qualify for nor require USL&HW protection. While they are working above navigable water, the employees do not meet the status test as they are not working with ships or water-going vessels.

Each state prescribes the benefits provided and must be listed for coverage to apply as for any other employee. USL&HW coverage does not apply to masters or crew members of vessels.

Nonappropriated Fund Instrumentalities Act Coverage Endorsement (WC 00 01 08A)

Civilians working on U.S.-based military installations are picked up by this endorsement. This includes non-military personnel working in exchange stores, movie theaters and other such operations. This endorsement extends the USL&HW Act benefits to these employees.

Defense Base Act Coverage Endorsement (WC 00 01 01A)

The defense base act is like the nonappropriated funds instrumentality act in that it extends USL&HW benefits to cover civilian employees working on military bases, however, there are some important differences.

- The defense base act covers civilian employees working in any capacity on military bases outside the continental United States. This includes Alaska and Hawaii.
- Covered operations include civilian employees of contractors or subcontractors engaged in public works projects with any U.S. governmental agency while outside the continental U.S. (i.e. Iraq and Afghanistan).
- Includes civilian employees working on contracts approved and funded under the Foreign Assistance Act outside the continental U.S.
- Coverage extends to employees working for U.S. employers providing welfare or similar services to

members of the armed forces outside the continental U.S. This includes such operations as the USO and Red Cross.

- Coverage under the defense base act applies to all civilian employees, not just U.S. citizens.

To trigger coverage, the endorsement must contain a description of the work and the location of the work.

Outer Continental Shelf Lands Act Coverage Endorsement (WC 00 01 09A)

"Outer continental shelfs" are submerged lands that lie seaward of various states subject to U.S. jurisdiction. USL&HW benefits are extended by describing the work and the endorsement must indicate in which state the location would be if the territorial boundaries extended to the outer continental shelf. This endorsement generally applies to employees engaged in the development, exploration or removal of natural resources (oil and gas) from the sea floor by use of a fixed platform.

Federal Coal Mine Health and Safety Act Coverage Endorsement (WC 00 01 02)

Federal Black Lung workers' compensation benefits are provided in the states listed in this endorsement, even in monopolistic states, in support of the Federal Coal Mine Health and Safety Act. Benefits are specified by Federal law.

Federal Employers' Liability Act Coverage Endorsement (WC 00 01 04A)

The oldest continuous operating workers' compensation act signed into law by President Taft in 1908 (See Chapter 1 – "Workers' Compensation History: The Great Tradeoff!"). Coverage is for railroad employees engaged in interstate commerce.

Maritime Coverage Endorsement (WC 00 02 01A)

This endorsement is used to extend workers' compensation and employers' liability coverage to employers required to provide maritime benefits under Admiralty Law, DHSA or the Jones Act to their employees but who do not have a Protection and Indemnity (P&I) policy or the P&I does not cover their entire operations. Coverage is triggered by describing the maritime operations that are to be insured which may include: limitations by size, ownership or name of the vessel; or limited by the names of waterways to be navigated by the vessel.

Voluntary Compensation Maritime Coverage Endorsement (WC 00 02 03)

Like the Maritime Coverage Endorsement, except this is used only when workers' compensation and employers' liability coverage is not required as there is less than the minimum number of employees. Same as the voluntary compensation endorsement used for non-maritime employees. The endorsement extends workers' compensation and employers' liability protection. Employees are covered by naming or describing the vessel to which they are assigned.

Chapter 13

Nonemployee 'Employees:' The Borrowed Servant Doctrine

"The vital test in determining whether a workman furnished by [the primary employer] is a servant of [the special employer] is whether they (the employee(s)) are subject to the "special employer's" control or right of control not only with regard to the work to be done but also with regard to the employee's manner of performing it." This paraphrase (changed to remove specificities) of the 1935 Pennsylvania Supreme Court's ruling in *Venezia v. Philadelphia Electric Company* has been the basis upon which questions, suits and claims involving supposed borrowed servants have been answered, decided and settled.

Workers' compensation coverage, as has been detailed, is to be the sole remedy for the injured employee and a protection against lawsuits for the employer (except in cases of egregious acts). The next several paragraphs will attempt to define who the "employer" is or may be — with a particular emphasis on the "borrowed servant doctrine."

Three 'Employers'

"Employer" has been inversely defined or delineated in earlier chapters by defining the "employee." Indirectly defining an employer can lead to misclassification of, or simply missed, employments leaving gaps in protection that could have been avoided if the relationship was recognized and properly managed up front. Employee-employer relationships presuppose certain duties and responsibilities upon each party; such a relationship can exist outside the usual and customarily understood context. Understanding how status as the employer can be created will allow the client and its agent the opportunity to manage the risk before the injury occurs. Employer status can be created in one of three ways.

- As primary/direct or de facto employer
- As statutory/de jure employer
- As a "special employer"

Primary/Direct or De Facto Employer

Direct employment is the traditional and most common employer-employee relationship. Status as a direct or primary employer is generally created via a contract of hire. Such contract may either be a formal written contract or an understood contract that follows negotiations, the employer's offer of employment and the employee's acceptance. All or nearly all direct employer-employee relationships share the same rights and operate in essentially the same manner (the following is not an all-inclusive list).

- The right to hire and fire any employee (as allowed by state law) is vested solely in the direct employer.

- Direct/primary employers exercise or have the right to exercise absolute control over their employee. Work hours, work methods and work location are all controlled by the direct/primary employer.
- Employees of direct employers generally do not or are not necessarily allowed to work for anyone other than the direct employer without the employer's express permission or at the employer's direction.
- Remuneration is paid by direct employers, whether a sole proprietor, partner, corporation or other entity, on a regularly scheduled basis via either a salary, commission, piecework basis or some other means. This is usually the employee's sole source (or primary source) of individual income.
- If the employer provides employee benefits, direct employees are eligible to receive and can reasonably expect these benefits.
- Applicable taxes are withheld from the worker's paycheck.
- Employees of direct employers are generally eligible to receive state and/or federally mandated unemployment benefits if they do lose their job.

A de facto employer is an employer "in fact or in reality." Employees often referred to as independent contractors are "in fact" employees. Employers may try to dodge federal and state employment laws, withholding requirements or the providing of benefits by classifying factual employees as independent contractors. The degree of control exercised by the employer (as delineated above) often influences the worker's classification as either a true independent contractor or a de facto employee.

The IRS applies a much more lenient definition of independent contractor than does the insurance industry, particularly workers' compensation carriers. Not withholding taxes and operating under a separate entity name (with potentially a few other qualifications) may be all that is required for the IRS to consider a worker an independent contractor.

However, workers' compensation rules are more stringent regarding the true nature and classification of a particular worker. The higher the degree of control over the worker, the more likely he will be considered an employee rather than an independent contractor. "Control" is defined later.

Direct and de facto employers are charged with providing workers' compensation benefits as prescribed by individual state law and discussed in previous chapters. An employer's violation of such requirements can result in criminal charges, fines and penalties (varying by state). Employers that lend or lease their direct employees to another employer (the special employer) are generally not relieved of their duty to provide workers' compensation coverage; this will depend on the contract if one exists. Knowing which direct employees remain the employer's responsibility allows better planning of the workers' compensation protection.

Statutory and De Jure Employees

Statutory or de jure employers are created by force of law.
Chapters 7 (Who Qualifies as an Employee in Workers'
Compensation Law) and 8 (The General Contractors'
Responsibility to Provide Protection) detailed the statutory
relationships that create employer-employee relationships. De
jure and statutory can be used nearly synonymously as part of
this discussion; de jure is defined to mean "by right or
according to the law." The employer is not the direct employer
or even necessarily "related" to the statutory employee but
becomes the employer of record by a vote of the legislature and
sometimes the findings of a court.

General contractors hiring uninsured subcontractors
become the statutory or de jure employers of the uninsured
subcontractor's employees and are thus legally responsible to
provide or arrange for workers' compensation benefits to be
paid to an injured worker. Forty-four states have codified this
relationship.

Any worker injured while in the course and scope of
employment for a statutory (de jure) employer must be
extended the same protection and benefits as those owed to
the employees of the direct employer. Indemnification and
hold harmless agreements between a general contractor and a
subcontractor can create a relationship that must be managed
via endorsement to the workers' compensation policy.

Special Employer

Control and the right of control is the overriding and deciding factor when analyzing the "borrowed servant doctrine." Does the "special employer" have the absolute right to control the actions of the worker? As stated previously, control only over the work being done is not sufficient; before status as a special employer can be assigned, the right of control must also encompass the manner in which the work is performed.

Classification as a "special employer" is the third means by which an employer-employee relationship can be created. Of the three, this is the most unique as it is not created by a direct contract of hire or even by a statutory requirement; this relationship and the responsibilities that accompany it are born almost solely out of the right of control.

Defining 'Control'

Employer-employee relationships impose specific duties and responsibilities upon each party. Employers are charged with many duties, among these are providing a safe and healthy work environment, making sure the correct tools are available to complete the assigned tasks, confirming that employees are properly trained and assuring that funds are available to cover the medical costs and/or lost wages should an injury occur (as per relevant statute). Employees, likewise, owe to their employer specific responsibilities; including the duty to do the job that is assigned to them and to do it to the best of their ability and with the best interest of their employer in mind.

Special employer situations under the "borrowed servant doctrine" are no different. Employer duty and employee responsibility are present, but such duties and responsibilities arise strictly from the right of control as has been repeatedly pointed out in the opening paragraphs.

Each governmental body with an interest in this relationship and the insurance industry for its own purposes apply specific tests when working to establish whether a particular worker is due protection under the "borrowed servant doctrine." All of these interested parties list the "right of control" as one factor in the list of tests to be applied; but "control" itself is not defined by the individual tests, its definition is drawn and applied from other sources.

- The entity or person controls the manner in which the work is performed. Controlled workers are taken step-by-step through the process with the person in control confirming or providing the necessary training to complete each step leading to the desired outcome.
- The place of performance is delineated by the entity or person with control.
- The time of performance is mandated. The worker is expected to show up at specified times and work a set number of hours (with breaks for rest and lunch). When such specific period is over, the worker is free to leave.

- Details of the performance are mandated by the entity in control. The necessary tools, supplies and work areas are provided by the person or entity in control. The finished product must meet the controlling entity's standards.
- The person supervising the worker is a direct employee of the entity or person that hired the worker.
- The work is being done exclusively for the entity that hired the worker (although the employer may turn over the finished product to another person or entity). Essentially, the worker is benefiting only the employer's business operation.

Absent sufficient evidence to the contrary, the original (direct) employer is presumed to retain control. But once the weight of the evidence based on the markers above conclusively shifts control to the "special employer," then the remaining "borrowed servant doctrine" tests can be scrutinized to determine if a "doctrinal" employer-employee relationship exists.

Other Borrowed Servant Tests

States and the federal government apply specific tests to determine if a particular worker qualifies as a "borrowed servant" and the employer as a "special employer." The majority of these tests revolve around the question of control. The insurance industry, thanks to Lex Larson and his "Larson's Workers' Compensation," marries the right of control detailed above with the various other tests to conceive and produce a three-part test to determine a worker's status as a borrowed servant and the employer's status as that of a special employer.

1. Has the employee made a contract of hire, express or implied, with the special employer? In essence, has the direct employer volunteered or directed the employee to work for the special employer and has the employee agreed to such assignment?
2. Is the work being done essentially that of the special employer (as discussed under the right of control)?
3. Does the special employer have the right to control the details of the work?

If all of those three questions are answered in the affirmative, then the employer is almost certainly a special employer and the employee a borrowed servant. There are other tests not contemplated by Larson that may need to be or will be considered by the court to absolutely prove special employer and borrowed servant status.

- Does the presumed special employer have the right to discharge the worker? If so, that evidences a borrowed servant.
- Who has the obligation to pay the employee? If the employee is paid by the borrowing employer, this is more proof of "special employer" status.
- What is the course of dealings between the direct employer and the presumed special employer? Is there

a contractual relationship or requirement? Employer-employee status can potentially be created by contract.

- Is the lent employee a specialist? And does the presumed special employer have the skill or knowledge to supervise the manner in which the work is being performed? This is a "negative test." If the borrowing employer does not have the ability or skill necessary, the lent worker will likely not be considered a borrowed servant since one cannot control what one does not understand and cannot do; thus the individual is not a putative employee but a specialist.

Combining and analyzing the right of control, Larson's three-prong test and the four other distinguishing test factors will produce as nearly as possible a definitive answer to the question of "special employer" and a resulting "borrowed servant." Special employers owe the same duties to their borrowed servants as they do to any direct employee. An employer-employee relationship is created that must be managed from both a human resources and a risk management angle.

Borrowed Servants

There are only a few work/employment situations that may lead to or lend themselves to special employer and borrowed servant situations. While this is not an all-inclusive list, these are the most common situations.

- **Temporary staffing operations**: The employee works for a temporary staffing company that "leases" the worker to other entities to fulfill short-term or maybe even long-term employment needs. This is not to be confused with an employee leasing operation such as a PEO; that is a wholly different arrangement with different risk management concerns and solutions (detailed in Chapter 15). The contract between the staffing firm and the employer may require the staffing firm to provide the workers' compensation coverage even though the leasing employer is, by all tests, the special employer.

- **Property managers required by the property owner to extend workers' compensation protection to the employees actively managing the property.**

- **Employee hired by the direct employer to work exclusively on or at the special employer's location or job site**. *White v. Bethlehem Steel* (U.S. Court of Appeals decision in 2000) addressed this issue. The employer (C.J. Langenfelder & Son Inc.) leased his equipment and employees to Bethlehem Steel. One of the employees had worked for Langenfelder for 26 years but had worked nearly exclusively at Bethlehem for his entire tenure. The employee was injured on the job; he collected the benefits due him from Langenfelder, but then sued Bethlehem Steel. The court found that since Bethlehem met all the requirements, it was the special employer and White was a borrowed servant. The employee-employer relationship blocked White's ability to sue Bethlehem since workers' compensation is the sole remedy in the employer-employee relationship. Such a relationship could also result from an accounting firm having an employee who works exclusively for one client and, in fact, has a desk at the client's office and reports there daily without going to the employer's location; or a computer/software company that keeps an employee on-site on a full-time basis for a large client; etc.

- **Contractual relationships between a general contractor and subcontractor.** Indemnification and hold harmless requirements may result in the general contractor becoming a special employer, especially in third party-over suits. As detailed in an earlier chapter the subcontractor or sub-subcontractor (and on down) could be held financially responsible for suits against a third party made by an injured employee, even if that employee received all the benefits due and did not sue the employer. Contractual relationships can potentially create a special employer exposure.

The Workers' Compensation Solution?

Primary employers may not be relieved of their duty to provide workers' compensation benefits to employees who are considered borrowed servants of a special employer. In fact, a contractual relationship may exist between the direct employer and the special employer specifically stating that coverage is to be maintained by the direct employer. The point thus far has been to spotlight the need for agents to discover these relationships (be they overt or hidden in a contract) and offer a potential solution to the client and even the client's customer (maybe winning a new account due to being so detail-oriented).

The Alternate Employer Endorsement (WC 00 03 01A) is designed to extend coverage when employees are considered the "borrowed servants" of a special employer. It is attached to the direct employer's policy, naming the special employer thus extending protection from the employer's policy to the putative employer.

All four of the above "borrowed servant" examples are eligible for the Alternate Employer Endorsement per the endorsement instructions. However, the instructions are only theoretical in nature and underwriting approval is not guaranteed; it may not even be likely.

- **Temporary staffing firms**. Underwriters willing to provide coverage, from the outset, for a temporary staffing firm will likely understand the need for this coverage and agree to provide this endorsement to all clients under the contract. If, however, the underwriter is unwilling to name the special employer (the lessee) as an alternate employer, the special employer may need to attach the Multiple Coordinated Policy

Endorsement (WC 00 03 23) to the workers' compensation policy. This endorsement extends benefits to the leased employees rather than having to depend on the staffing firm for coverage. Agents writing coverage for the special employer need to be aware of the exposure and the availability of this endorsement.

- **Property management firms**. Again, underwriters may see and understand the need for this extension and agree to provide the endorsement when requested by the property owner.

- **Employees working almost exclusively on the property of another**. Underwriters may not be willing to extend such coverage as they may not see the need. If there is a contract, agents may be able to convince the underwriter to meet the contractual requirement.

- **Contractual risk transfer.** It is unlikely an underwriter will ever allow the use of this endorsement in a contractual situation; doing so would be akin to naming the upper tier contractor as an additional insured (but is not as broad in that it only provides a means to finance the suit not protect against it). But the unwillingness of the underwriter to give this endorsement, especially if the CGL underwriter has altered the definition of an "insured contract," may create a big out-of-pocket expense for the lower tier contractor. The lower tier contractor highlighted in

"Contractual Risk Transfer Done Right with the Wrong Results" could have been out-of-pocket $2 million if the CGL redefined "insured contract."

If the underwriter will not extend protection, the special employer should be notified that its workers' compensation policy may be called upon to provide the required benefits due these borrowed servants. Likewise, agents whose clients may be considered the special employer need to advise them of the possibility that such protection may be required and that an accompanying additional premium may result from the additional employees (see Chapter 12).

Extra-Insurance (Outside) Protection Provided by the Borrowed Servant Doctrine

Being considered a borrowed servant may extend unexpected protection to the worker and his direct employer apart from any workers' compensation matter. Such protection arises out of the sole remedy protection living in workers' compensation statutes.

Many, if not most, borrowed servant suits researched while constructing this chapter had little or nothing to do with workers' compensation coverage per se, but rather dealt with the injured party's rights to sue the person who caused their injury and that person's direct employer.

Essentially, if the person causing the injury is judged to be, "doctrinally," a borrowed servant, he is considered an employee of the special employer. As a "fellow employee" of the injured person he cannot be held personally liable for the injured person (provided this person did not act egregiously or intentionally) because workers' compensation is the sole source of recovery for injury arising out of and in the course of employment, however caused.

Likewise, the direct employer of the borrowed servant cannot be held vicariously liable for the actions of its direct employee since that employee is under the control of another entity. The theory of respondeat superior (Latin for "let the master answer") applies to the special employer not the direct employer due to the finding of fact regarding who has control of the employee. Since the special "master" has already responded by paying workers' compensation benefits, the direct "master" has no need and cannot be compelled to contribute.

Chapter 14

Work Comp for PEOs and Their Client/Employers

Professional employer organizations (PEOs) began their rise after the adoption of the Tax Equity and Fiscal Responsibility Act of 1982 cleared a path for the creation and expansion of such entities. Over 700 professional employer organizations operate in all 50 states. According to the National Association of Professional Employer Organizations, between two and three million employees work under a PEO arrangement and PEOs as an industry earned $61 billion in gross revenues in 2007 (gross revenues are the total payrolls plus the fees charged by the PEO).

PEO contracts are co-employment arrangements whereby the professional employer organization and the client with which it contracts both retain some right of control over the individual worker or workers collectively. Such relationship is wholly different than a leased employee or the use of a borrowed servant as detailed in Chapter 14. Leased employees and borrowed servants are under the absolute control of the special employer. Co-employment vests responsibility and control with both parties to the contract.

According to The National Association of Professional Employer Organizations (NAPEO) (http://www.napeo.org)

Web site, a PEO establishes a contractual relationship with its clients so that the PEO takes on certain rights, responsibilities, and risks.

- The PEO may assume certain employment responsibilities for specified purposes regarding the workers at the client locations.
- The PEO may reserve a right of direction and control of the employees with respect to particular matters.
- The PEO shares or allocates employment responsibilities with the client in a manner consistent with the client maintaining its responsibility for its product or service.
- The PEO remits wages and withholdings of the client's workers.
- The PEO issues Form W-2s for the compensation paid under its Employer Identification Number.
- The PEO reports, collects and deposits employment taxes with local, state and federal authorities.

(Editor's Note: The information above was collected from the NAPEO website at https://www.napeo.org/what-is-a-peo/about-the-peo-industry/what-is-co-employment and was current as of this edition's publishing date.)

NCCI and PEO Arrangements

NCCI has continued to monitor the workers' compensation issues and problems created when employers choose to join a

PEO. A 2005 report printed in NCCI's *Workers' Compensation Issues Report* delineates and briefly discusses many of the continuing issues.

- Experience Modification Calculations: Most states require the PEO to individually monitor and report the claims experience of each individual client. The purpose is to thwart the efforts of employers with bad experience to escape their problems by joining a PEO for a couple of years then coming back out and starting over. Since individual experience must be monitored and reported, the employer's experience mod will be correct based on its experience; it will not get a 1.0 when it leaves the PEO unless that is what it has earned.

- The ability of executive officers to exclude themselves (if allowed by law); and/or the ability of sole proprietors or partners to include themselves (if allowed by law). The ability to include or exclude members of an LLC (based on the applicable state law).

- Problems that might arise if the employer/client hires an uninsured subcontractor. Is the PEO's workers' compensation carrier required to pay as the statutory employer?

- Problems that arise out of PEOs being insured in state assigned risk pools.

- Are the proper endorsements in place? For example, NCCI states in this article that the Alternate Employer Endorsement is not intended for use in co-employment situations. However, without using this endorsement there is a problem when trying to effectuate and confirm the proper dovetailing of coverage between the employer/client and the PEO (detailed below).

The report from NCCI specifically lists and highlights more problems than those listed above.

Insuring PEOs

Four endorsements are available for use in co-employment situations (an additional form may be necessary depending on the jurisdiction). Two are client-specific and two are designed to be attached to the PEO's policy. Contractual agreement between the PEO and the employer regarding which entity is responsible for providing workers' compensation benefits govern which endorsements are used.

Employer/Client is responsible for providing workers' compensation

When the employer/client is contractually responsible for providing benefits, two endorsements dovetail to provide the necessary or required workers' compensation benefits:

- **Labor Contractor Endorsement (WC 00 03 20 A).** This endorsement is attached to the client's (the leasing employer's) policy. Attachment of this endorsement extends benefits to the leased employees from the employer's policy and essentially provides additional insured status to the scheduled PEO. The use of this endorsement is coupled with the next endorsement.

- **Labor Contractor Exclusion Endorsement (WC 00 03 21).** Attached to the PEO's workers' compensation policy, this exclusionary endorsement excludes coverage for employees leased to the client(s) scheduled in the form. This endorsement is used when the client leases employees on an "other-than-short term" basis and such client is charged with providing the workers' compensation benefits.

PEO is responsible for providing workers' compensation protection

As above, two endorsements, one attached to the employer's/client's policy and the second to the PEO's, work in tandem to assure that coverages mesh as per the contractual agreement that the PEO will extend workers' compensation benefits to the workers.

- **Employee Leasing Client Exclusion Endorsement (WC 00 03 22).** Attach this endorsement to the employer's/client's workers' compensation policy to exclude the extension of workers' compensation benefits to employees leased on a long-term basis from the labor contractor (PEO) scheduled in the policy. Only used when the PEO is responsible for providing coverage. The employer/client must confirm that the PEO attaches the next endorsement.

- **Professional Employer Organization (PEO) Extension Endorsement (WC 00 03 20 B).** Workers' compensation and employers' liability benefits extend exclusively from the PEO when this endorsement is attached to the PEO's policy. This extension only applies to employees leased to the client(s) listed on the schedule.

- Alternate **Employer Endorsement (WC 00 03 01 A).** Although NCCI states that this endorsement is not properly used in co-employment situations and even the form itself does not contemplate its use in these relationships; if the insured is located in a state that has not approved the PEO Extension Endorsement discussed above, this may be the only way to extend coverage from the PEO's form to protect the employer/client. This endorsement is attached to the PEO's policy naming the employer/client as the alternate employer. The use of this form in co-employment contracts is not recommended and should be avoided if possible.

Workers' Compensation Policies for Employers in PEOs

As evidenced by the above discussion, it is absolutely essential that the employer/client have in place a workers' compensation policy even when the PEO is contractually providing coverage. Since both entities are legally employers and in fact are the "employers of record," such contractual arrangement does not preclude the necessity of coverage.

Exposure to a workers' compensation claim still exists if an uninsured subcontractor is hired, if there are employees hired outside of the leasing contract (temporary workers, etc.) and other potential gaps in protection as studied and monitored by NCCI. And while it may seem like a weak argument, without a workers' compensation policy in force, the employer/client has nothing to which these endorsements can attach attesting that coverage is extended from another party.

Lastly, if the PEO loses its coverage or suddenly goes out of business, the employer is in violation of the law until coverage can be placed. Certainly many employers have received notice that the PEO with which they were contracted is no longer in business. When I owned my agency I had a PEO (I bought it with that set up, I did not create the relationship). I received a fax one evening stating that the PEO would cease to operate the next day; workers' compensation coverage had to be placed, immediately, and I became responsible for payroll administration and other functions inherent in human resources management.

Employers should carry the workers' compensation policy even if it must be set up using "If Any" payrolls. The cost is very low for the protection it provides. A central theme of risk management is "don't risk a lot for a little." The small premium may avoid big problems.

Chapter 15
Combinability of Insureds

Consolidating separate legal entities' loss experience to develop a common experience modification factor has the potential to cause confusion for the client and sometimes the agent. Clients may view such mixing of loss experience due simply to common majority ownership as less than reasonable, especially if the commonly-owned entities substantially differ with regard to the relative hazard presented (i.e. the owners of a heavy equipment contracting company purchase a marina).

Combinability rules do not merely marry the experience of entities that are currently in operation and related via common majority ownership, they also assure that owners do not avoid their historically poor loss records simply by closing down one entity and reopening and operating under another corporate name. Most agents would agree that such a stunt is unethical at best and may actually be considered fraud. Changing the name of the operation does not change the operational methods of the owner(s).

Understanding combinability rules necessitates a basic understanding of the theory and practice behind the calculation of experience modification factors. Following is a brief synopsis of experience modification calculations.

Calculating Experience Modification Factors

Workers' compensation loss costs are calculated and charged based on the average expected losses for that particular business classification. All insureds in the same hazard class (based on the assigned code) are charged the same basic loss cost (individual carriers apply conversion factors to these loss costs to develop their individual rates). However, not all insureds within a particular hazard class operate in the same manner, nor does each experience the same losses. To adjust for these differences in operation and loss histories, a method had to be created allowing for premium/rate differentiation between the above average, average and below average insureds within any particular hazard class code.

Experience modification factors (experience mods) allow such "customizing" and individualization of the workers' compensation premium. Basing the standard premium on the insured's unique loss history allows the class' average rates to remain relatively constant and the subject insured to be rewarded or punished based on its own experience (rather than be subject solely to the experience of the group).

"Stop loss" limits used as part of the experience mod calculation makes loss frequency weightier than loss severity. One large claim will not damage an experience mod factor as drastically as three small claims in a single experience period (the "experience period" is usually the three years ending 12 months prior to the policy effective date – a 6/1/19 mod would apply the experience for the three years ending 6/1/18).

Calculating experience modification factors is far more complicated than presented in three short paragraphs. Mod calculations are a function of expected losses, actual losses, payrolls, class averages, loss limits (medical only vs. medical plus indemnity) and formulary factors applied by NCCI (or the applicable rating bureau) to all such collected data. Chapter 18 provides a detailed analysis of experience modification calculations.

Knowing and understanding that experience modification factor calculations allow for the reward or punishment of individual employers allows one to more clearly view the need for loss experience combinability. Employers should not be freed of their premium responsibility simply due to legal structure. And rarely are majority-owned entities not interrelated such that employees work for multiple entities even though they appear to be operating for just one employer in the course and scope of their daily duties (combinability avoids some of the problems created by the borrowed servant doctrine).

A Case for Combinability Rules

Owners theoretically run each and every operation (past and present) in essentially the same manner and with the same attitudes. An employer that is concerned with safety and strives to provide the best equipment and training will likely always act the same with each entity. Likewise, employers looking for the easiest and cheapest way out will likely continue down the same path in the future. Combinability rules are, to some extent, based around these theories.

- Employers that operate in the supposed best interest of their employees should have all their entities (current and future) rewarded due to such attitude. Commonly owned operations will likely be managed in the same manner and the same care and concern is expected to be showed for all employees (regardless of the hazard of the operation).
- If an employer allows unsafe operations in one entity, it is reasonable to postulate that such attitude will carry over to the new entity and all commonly owned entities (current and future). Employers not operating (or not appearing to operate) in the best interest of their employees should be subject to their past (or current) experience.

Past actions are not a guarantee of future actions, but they stand as a very good indicator. To not reward or punish allows employers/owners to act with impunity, knowing that as long as no law is broken, all that is necessary to escape a poor loss history is the killing off of an old and birthing a new corporation.

Without the ability to combine loss histories, workers' compensation carriers would potentially be victims of inadequate premiums. In like manner, average and above average risks would be victimized by higher premiums than necessary. The "average loss cost" balance would be tilted, and all employers would likely see an increase in their rates rather than just the ones that "earned" the increase. Rate predictability and possibly rate adequacy may be compromised without combinability rules.

Granted, there are exceptions to every rule such as is demonstrated by the employer that had a hiccup in its loss history not indicative of its past. Not every injury can be avoided, even with top-notch safety and training, bad "things" sometimes just happen. This is why there is underwriting discretion and the availability of rate credits and debits. A historically above-average employer with a bad year or two in their experience modification calculation can have the debit mod negated by a rate credit.

Conversely, an average or below average employer that has been fortunate can be debited to account for the increased hazard presented to the insured. Employers that do not practice or refuse to comply with recommended safety practices, as reported by the loss control department, can see their rates increased by a debit factor in anticipation of the increased potential for employee injury.

Combinability Guidelines

Common majority ownership is the basic rule of combinability. When the same person, group of persons or a corporation owns a majority interest in another entity, the owned entity's loss experience is combined with the owning entity to develop a common (combined) experience modification factor.

The combinability concept seems simple enough, however achieving "common majority ownership" can be accomplished in one of several relational constructs.

- **The corporation (a "legal person") owns a majority interest in other entities**. When Corp "A" owns a "majority interest" (this term will be defined in upcoming paragraphs) in Corp "B," the loss experience of both corporations is pooled to produce a single, combined experience modification factor.

- **The business' owner(s) ("natural person(s)") individually or collectively maintain majority interest in more than one entity**. If John holds majority interest in Corp "A" and he individually gains majority interest in Corp "B," the two entities are combined for experience rating. However, if John has majority interest in only one of the two entities, they are not combinable (i.e. John maintains 75 percent interest in Corp "A" but only 25 percent in Corp "B"). To continue, assume that John and Joe combine to own majority interest in Corp "A" and Corp "B;" common majority ownership exists, and the experience is combinable.

- **The corporation combines with some or all of its owners to hold a majority interest in another entity**. Corp "A" (again, a "legal person") maintains 30 percent interest in Corp "B;" John and Joe (100 percent owners of Corp "A") hold 25 percent of Corp "B." The combined ownership of the legal person and the natural persons result in common majority ownership (55 percent) of Corp "B" making the two entities combinable.

- **The business owns a majority interest in another entity which, itself, owns or owned a majority interest in a third entity currently operating or which operated in the last five years**.

This is not an exhaustive list of relationships that can lead to combinability of loss experience; it is but a representation of the most common. These guidelines are subject to NCCI and/or individual state rating bureau interpretations. Agents, brokers and carriers should use these descriptions only for informational purposes as final determination rests in these other advisory bodies.

Natural and Legal Persons

Notice the repeated use of the natural and legal person(s) concept in the above paragraphs. Common majority interest can be created when a single "person" or a group of "persons" combine to hold a majority interest in multiple entities. It matters little whether the owners of other entities are natural persons, legal persons or a combination. Nor does it matter how they combine to create common majority interest between or among two or more entities.

Legal persons are generally created by the actions and desires of natural persons. Some legal persons are owned by one or only a few natural persons (a small business) while some are "owned" by many shareholders (traded on the stock exchanges). Natural and legal persons are defined as follows.

- **Natural person:** A flesh and blood human being. In workers' compensation the employer is a natural person(s) in sole proprietorships and partnerships. Managers and members of an LLC are viewed as natural persons in a majority of states making these persons the employers.
- **Legal person (a.k.a. juridical person):** A legal fiction, a "person" created by statute and born with the filing of articles of incorporation. These legal persons are given the right to own property, sue and be sued. Corporations are legal persons and several states consider LLCs a legal person.

'Majority Interest'

Majority interest is created when the same person or group of persons combine to own more than 50 percent of an entity. But majority interest can be created in many ways.

- An entity or persons (as detailed above) owns the majority of the voting stock of another entity.
- Both entities share a majority of the same owners (if there is no voting stock). Generally these are natural persons that own multiple entities.

- If neither of the above applies, majority interest is created if a majority of the board is common between two or among several entities.
- Participation of each general partner in the profits of the partnership (limited partners are excluded).
- When ownership interest is held by an entity as a fiduciary (excludes a debtor in possession, a trustee under an irrevocable trust or a franchisor).

Combinability Conclusion

Based on and applying the above common majority interest rules, the possibility exists for more than one combination of common related entities. Deciding which combination of entities applies is based on the following two rules (presented in order of importance).

1. Which combination involves the most entities?
2. If the above does not apply, the combination is based on the group that produces the largest estimated standard premium.

Regardless of how a group is created and combined, no entity's experience will be used more than once.

Finally, although separate entities may be combinable for experience modification calculation, this does not exclude them from having separate workers' compensation policies. Separate legal entities are entitled (and really required) to be written on separate workers' compensation policies; combinability rules exist merely to assure that loss histories are not escaped by the creation of multiple legal entities or the closing of one and opening of a new one.

Chapter 16
Audit Rules and Guidelines

Workers' compensation coverage is initially priced on an estimated basis. The insured estimates payrolls (and sometime class codes) at the beginning of the policy period for the upcoming year on which the insurance carrier charges a premium using the prescribed rates. After the close of the policy year, the insurance carrier desires to firm up the numbers to confirm collection of the actual premium earned for the actual exposure insured. This "firming-up" is known as the premium audit (see Chapter 12).

Premium audits are addressed by Part Five, paragraph G., of NCCI's Workers' Compensation and Employers' Liability Insurance Policy. The form reads as follows.

> **G. Audit:** *You will let us examine and audit all your records that relate to this policy These records include ledgers, journals, registers, vouchers, contracts, tax reports, payroll and disbursement records, and programs for storing and retrieving data. We may conduct the audits during regular business hours during the policy period and within **three years** after the policy period ends. Information developed by audit will be used to determine final premium. Insurance rate service*

organizations have the same rights we have under this provision.

Premium Basis

Premium, with rare exception, is based on payroll, also known as remuneration. Below are the common remuneration inclusions and exclusions.

Remuneration Included:

- Wages/Salaries
- Commissions: if on draw, and draw is greater than commissions earned, use the entire amount of the draw
- Bonuses, unless awarded for individual invention or discovery
- Overtime: one-third of amount is subtracted from the total amount (one-half if it is double-time pay)
- Pay for holidays, vacations, or periods of sickness
- Pay for time not worked (i.e., paid for an 8-hour day when only 7 hours worked)
- Pay for travel time to or from work or specific job site
- Employer payments of amounts otherwise required by law (i.e., Statutory insurance, Social Security, etc.)
- Contributions to a savings plan or vacation fund required by a union contract
- IRS Qualified Salary Reduction Plan (i.e. 401K) (refers to the employee's contribution and any qualified agreement between the employer and the employee to pay into a retirement plan in lieu of direct wages)

- Employee Savings Plans: only the amount given by the employee, not the employer's match, if any
- Contributions to an IRA made by the employee
- Payment on any basis other than time worked such as piecework, incentive plans or profit-sharing plans
- Payment or allowance for tools
- Value of housing/lodging
- Value of meals
- Substitutes for money (merchandise certificates, store credit, etc.)

Remuneration Excluded:

- Tips and other gratuities
- Payments by employer to Group Insurance or Pension Plans (employer matching)
- Special rewards for individual invention or discovery
- Severance pay
- Pay for those on active military duty
- Employee discounts
- Expense reimbursements
- Money for meals for overtime work
- Work uniform allowance
- Sick pay paid by a third party
- Employer-provided perks (company autos, incentive vacations, memberships)

Special Payroll Considerations: Sole Proprietors, Partners, LLC Members and Executive Officers

Actual payroll for each employee is used in the calculation of the final workers' compensation premium with just a few common exceptions. Sole proprietors, partners, LLC members and executive officers are treated differently than regular employees.

Sole proprietors and partners in states that allow these persons to choose to be subject to the workers' compensation law and covered by the policy are generally assigned a payroll regardless of their actual gross income. This amount is adjusted annually to account for inflation and other cost of living factors. Each state which allows these individuals to "opt in" assigns its own payroll limit (it is not the same throughout the country).

Executive officers are generally subject to an upper and lower weekly payroll limit rather than a set annual payroll like sole proprietors and partners. If, for instance, the minimum weekly payroll assignable to an executive officer is $331 per week ($17,212 per year) with a maximum weekly payroll of $1,300 per week ($67,600 per year); an executive officer paid $300,000 per year will appear on the audit at $67,600 per year. Remember, not all officers are executive officers. Executive officers are generally limited to the president or CEO, the CFO and certain levels of vice presidents. The delineation is a function of the articles of incorporation and can vary from entity to entity.

Members and managers of an LLC are, once again, subject to state laws. Some states treat these individuals as sole proprietors/partners while others view them as executive officers. The subject law should be reviewed to confirm how these individuals are classified and thus how payrolls will be assigned based on the descriptions above. Likewise, proper assignment of the founders/organizers of a professional association (PA) will be subject to individual state statutes.

There are three operational and actuarial reasons for such payroll limitations.

1. Getting paid more does not increase the likelihood that an injury will occur. A plumbing company executive officer actually engaged in plumbing work and earning $150,000 per year is no more likely to get hurt than the $15 per hour "plumber's helper." In fact, he is probably less likely to get hurt due to experience and personal interest. The amount of pay does not increase the chance of injury.

2. Medical costs, theoretically, don't fluctuate based on the individual's income. A broken leg costs the same to set for the owner and the hourly employee.

3. Indemnity payments are limited to a minimum and maximum in each state. As discussed in Chapter 5, each state sets the minimum and maximum weekly indemnity benefits. If the maximum that an injured executive or employee can receive in any given year is $75,000 (just for example sake), it is not reasonable to expect the insured to pay a premium based on a gross

income of $200,000. This operational rule is combined with the previous two to limit the amount of payroll assignable to these special classes of people.

Governing Classification and the Single Enterprise Rule

Once final payrolls are calculated, a "Governing Classification" is assigned to the employer. The governing classification is generally based on the class code generating the largest payroll; rarely the highest rated code is used as the governing class (usually only used in construction-related operations if used at all). All employee payrolls, with certain exclusions and exceptions expounded upon later, are assigned to the governing classification.

The governing classification is intended to represent the exposure created by the overall operational business, not the exposure of each individual employee. Applying the single enterprise rule, the governing classification is designed to anticipate all the normal activities conducted by a particular operation or business. For example, a steel fabrication plant may have employees that rivet, others that bend and shape the steel, others that paint the finished product and still others that add braces and brackets. Even though there are different exposures presented by each of these operations, all payroll is assigned to the same class code.

Further, there are some activities a business conducts that appear to be so unrelated to the primary operations as to require or allow separate classification be assigned. However,

NCCI considers some of these activities to be an integral part of the business' operations thus the payroll of the individuals engaged in these activities is included in the governing classification. These are the "General Inclusions".

- Employees that work in a restaurant, cafeteria or commissary run by the business for use by the employees (this does not apply to such establishments at construction sites).
- Employees manufacturing containers such as boxes, bags, can or cartons for the employer's use in shipping its own products.
- Staff working in hospitals or medical facilities operated by the employer for use by the employees.
- Maintenance or repair shop employees.
- Printing or lithography employees engaged in printing for the employer's own products.

Payroll for any employee engaged in the above activities is assigned to the governing classification.

Exceptions to the Governing Classification Rules

There are four exceptions to the governing classification and single enterprise rules.

- The "Standard Exception" classifications
- The "Interchange of Labor" rules
- The "General Exclusion" classes

- Employers eligible for classification under the "Multiple Enterprise" rule

'Standard Exception' Classifications

Some duties/activities are so common to most businesses and may be so far outside the operational activities of the entity that employees engaged in these positions are considered exceptions to the governing classification rules. Payroll for these "standard exception" classes of employees is subtracted from the governing classification and assigned to the applicable standard exception code and rated separately from the governing class.

- Clerical Employees – Class Code 8810
- Clerical Telecommuter - Class Code 8871
- Drafting Employees - Class Code 8810
- Salespersons - Class Code 8742
- Drivers - Class Code 7380

For a particular employee or group of employees to qualify for assignment into one of the standard exception classifications, he/she must be physically separated from the operative hazards of the business by means of walls, floors, partitions or counters. Such separation requirement does not negate the assignment of an employee to a standard exception class if he is only entering the area of operation to conduct duties consistent with his class code; such as a clerical employee entering the operations area to deliver paychecks.

Standard exception classifications are not necessarily limited to these five class codes; some states utilize state-specific class codes that are also eligible for assignment as a standard exception. For example, Texas allows certain employees to be assigned to "Executive Officers NOC" (class code 8809) and the payroll for these employees is pulled out of the governing classification and rated as a standard exception.

Employees falling into a standard exception classification may not always be eligible for "standard exception" separation. Attention must be paid to the governing classification description; at times, the governing classification may state "...&..." or "...including...." If such wording appears, the payroll for the standard exception employee is included in the governing classification. The reason for such inclusion, the analogy of that particular operation requires the presence of the standard exception employees to accomplish the goals of such business. Here are a few examples of this.

- Farm: Nursery Employees & Drivers (Class Code 0005)
- Chemical manufacturing NOC - all operations & Drivers (Class Code 4829)
- Carpet, rug or upholstery cleaning & Drivers (Class Code 2585)
- Physicians & Clerical (Class Code 8832)
- Photographer - All employees & Clerical, Salespersons and Drivers (Class Code 4361)
- School: Professional Employees & Clerical (Class Code 8868)

Interchange of Labor

A second exception to the governing classification rule is the "interchange of labor" rule. The applicability of this rule varies by state; some states only allow its use in the construction, erection or stevedoring classes of business while other states permit the interchange of labor rule to apply to any type of business operation.

Interchange of labor rules allow a single employee's payroll to be split between or among several class codes that may be present within the operations. The advantage to the employer (premium payer) of such allowance is an ultimately lower premium. Without the interchange of labor rule, the employee's entire payroll would be assigned to the governing (likely highest rate) classification. With the interchange of labor rule in effect, the employer is charged based on the employee's actual exposure to injury.

For instance, an employee in the construction industry who does framing work (5645) and hardwood floor installation (5437) can see his payroll divided between these different operations and realize a reduction in premium provided the following specific provisions are met.

- All classifications used for an employee are appropriate to the job performed.
- Payroll records exist that allocate the employee's wages between/among the different classes. This requires an actual, dollar amount payroll split, a percentage of payroll is not allowed.

- The division of payroll is not available with any of the standard exception classifications (with the possible exception of the driver code).
- The operations/activities are not conducted on the same job site.

Continuing the above example using assigned risk rates of $25 for code 5645 and $14 for code 5437, an employee earning an annual payroll of $30,000 will cost the employer $7,500 if there is no interchange of labor. If, however, all the interchange of labor guidelines are met, and the employee's payroll is split as follows: $20,000 for framing and $10,000 for hardwood floor installation; the employee will only cost $6,400 in workers' compensation premium (ignoring expense constants, modification factors and debits or credits).

The interchange of labor rule is great for the employer due to the premium savings and is fair for the insurance carrier because exposures differ based on activity. When the employee is on scaffolding he is more like to suffer a severe injury than when installing flooring.

Employers and their agents must understand and take advantage of the interchange of labor rules allowed in each state. Large payrolls can greatly benefit from such splits thus agents should encourage detailed payroll records be kept and the audits should be checked closely.

General Exclusion Classifications

Some operational activities do not fit into the analogous assignment of the governing classification due to the unexpected existence of such an operation as part of a particular business. It is not reasonable to expect the hardware store code (8010) to pick up the exposure created by an onsite sawmill operation (2710) for example.

Such operations are known as "general exclusion" classes. General exclusion classes are listed separately on the workers' compensation policy and a separate rate (based on the class code) is charged for the employees within these classes of operations.

General exclusion classes are the opposite of "standard exception" classes. General exclusion classes are completely unexpected and not considered part of the analogy of the governing classification of an operation requiring separation to allow the insurer to garner the usually higher premium for the increased exposure. Standard exceptions represent operations common to most business and are of such minimal hazard that the insured should not be punished by having the payroll for these classes included in the governing classification, but should rather enjoy a lower premium for the reduced exposure.

Some operations and activities falling within the general exclusion classification follow.

- Employees working in aircraft operations
- Employees performing new construction or alterations

- Stevedoring employees
- Sawmill operation employees
- Employees working in an employer-owned daycare

Multiple Enterprise Rule

The single enterprise rule requires that all activities usual and customary to a particular operation be assigned to one "governing" class code (with the exceptions described above). However, a particular entity may conduct additional operations not usual or customary to such an enterprise; such disparate activities may allow the insured to qualify for the separation of payroll into multiple classifications under the "multiple enterprise rule."

A secondary operation producing a basic premium equal to or higher than the governing class code (the code generating the highest payroll) premium automatically qualifies for separation under the multiple enterprise rule with the only requirement being segregation of payrolls.

If, however, the basic premium generated by the secondary operation is less than the governing class code basic premium, four tests must be satisfied before the insured can make use of the multiple enterprise rule.

1. The operation is not commonly found within the operation of the subject insured's business.
2. The operation could each exist as a separate entity.
3. Financial records are kept separately for each operation.

4. The operations are physically separated by means of a partition, wall or placement in a separate building.

Such separation of payrolls may benefit the insured employer by a reduction in premium if the secondary enterprise carries a lower rate per $100 of payroll. Additionally, employers that qualify for separation of payrolls under the multiple enterprise rule may also be able to benefit from the application of the interchange of labor rule as presented above and based on the state.

ABCs of Premium Audits

There are specific guidelines that agents and the employer should apply to every audit. These are the "ABCs" of premium audits.

A: Always be there. A representative from the company familiar with the financial records and the operations of the company should be present at every audit. The auditor will likely have questions and unless someone is available to answer these questions and explain the financial documents, the auditor will have to make some potentially costly assumptions and/or mistakes. This duty should not be delegated to any member of the staff not intimately familiar with the business and its finances.

B: Be prepared. The auditor will need all the necessary financial records to conduct the audit and will likely ask for a tour of the facility. Prepare a place for the auditor to work and help them complete their job as quickly as possible. Some data that will need to be ready includes the following.

- <u>Payroll records</u>: Payroll journal and summary; 941s; state unemployment reports; an explanation and break out of overtime payments; and the general ledger.
- <u>Employee records</u>: Include a detailed description of job duties; the number of employees; employee hire and fire dates; and class code splits if applicable.
- <u>Cash disbursements</u>: Cost of and payments to subcontractors; cost of materials; and the cost of any casual labor hired.
- <u>Certificates of Insurance</u>: Make sure to supply current certificates of insurance covering the entire period of the audit or the entire period of time the contractor has worked for the insured. If the sub's policy renews in the middle of the audit period, a new certificate should be requested covering the remainder of the insured's policy period.
- <u>OCIP projects</u>: If the insured has been a part of any wrap-up, the auditor needs this information in order to remove the payroll from the calculation.

C: Copy of the auditor's work papers. Don't let the auditor leave without getting a copy of the audit work papers. This will allow the insured and the agent to review the audit and confirm that there are no errors BEFORE the audit is processed and billed (fixing it "after-the-fact" is more difficult).

D: Don't volunteer more information than asked. The auditor will ask questions, this is expected. Insureds should be advised to only answer the questions asked and not lead the auditor down a path that may be detrimental to the insured.

E: Exceptions to the single entity rule. The exceptions listed above should be capitalized on by the insured. Audits should, at the very minimum, contain at least one standard exception code. If the insured is eligible for any of the other payroll splits described above, those codes should also be included.

Knowing the rules and exceptions, giving the auditors everything they need to complete the audit quickly and following the above rules will increase the chances of a favorable audit.

Chapter 17

Audit Problems Leading to Additional Premiums

Let's dispense with the niceties and all attempts to eloquently ease into a discussion on the troubles surrounding workers' compensation audits. Rather let's jump right into the problem, assignment of "employee" status to non-employees. This is not the only problem, but this is where most additional premium headaches seem to originate.

Statutes in most jurisdictions are rather clear regarding who is and is not an employee, but auditors have taken it upon themselves, on many occasions, to assign an individual "employee" status in direct contradiction to statutory language; particularly when it comes to sole proprietors, partners, corporate officers, properly insured subcontractors and true independent contractors. Worse yet, different carriers' audit departments treat the same exposure in different ways, which leaves agents to guess on the outcome. Guessing usually ends with the client being stuck with an additional premium bill and the loss of a client.

There was one agent who was sued by his insured to recover the amount of the additional premium audit (in the neighborhood of $75,000 to $80,000) resulting from independent and statutorily exempt subcontractors being assigned "employee" status. The insured claimed the agent never advised him which workers might and might not be considered employees and thus the agent erred in his professional responsibility and duty to the insured. Even if no lawsuit had been filed, the client will likely move his coverage at renewal (or sooner), even if the audit is right.

Challenging an auditor's ruling seems to be a no-win proposition akin to tilting at windmills. Some underwriters have related that they cannot overrule the auditor; and even the states seem to be or choose to be impotent in a classification dispute.

Before completely ripping auditors apart, let's agree that good ones can be a valuable resource when working on a difficult account. Some company auditors will even take the time to help agents classify the insured (which could possibly help win an account). I have had occasion to establish an up-front agreement with the auditor regarding a particular insured's classification at audit. Auditors who go above and beyond need to be recognized to their managers and the manager's manager. Bosses generally hear nothing at all or bad reports, a good report will stand out in their mind and the auditor will be an ally later.

To be fair, the auditor's job is not always easy. Judging who is and is not an employee is not always clear. Several chapters in this book have tried to offer guidance, but even with this and other material, there are still gray areas. When there is a gray area, the auditor will go with the conservative approach and assign "employee" status. The bad part is the agent doesn't generally find out until receiving the angry call from the insured holding the audit bill in his hand. How the auditor is approached once the audit is contested will hopefully go a long way towards amiably rectifying any problems.

Regardless, the agent needs to protect himself or herself from the whims of the auditor or the sufficiency of gray area that may lead to an additional premium audit. Employee status in workers' compensation is a function of law, not a function of the policy, and since agents are not generally lawyers, the best they can do is make an educated interpretation, but even that might be wrong.

Stuart Powell CPCU, CIC, CLU, ARM, ChFC, AMIM, AAI, ARe, former vice president of Insurance Operations for the Independent Insurance Agents of North Carolina, crafted a letter for agents to send to their clients upon purchase or renewal of a workers' compensation policy. This well-written letter explains to the client what workers' compensation is, how it is priced, how employee status is determined and what will happen at audit.

The Letter

Insured Addressee
Business Name
Street Address
City, State, Zip

Re: Workers' Compensation Policy

Dear Client:

You recently purchased (renewed) a Workers' Compensation and Employers' Liability Insurance Policy. This policy is designed to support and comply with (this state's)Workers' Compensation Laws and to provide benefits as prescribed by statute to any injured employee whose injury or disease "arises out of and in the course and scope of" their employment.

Payroll generally determines the ultimate cost of coverage. Estimated payroll supplied by you at the beginning of the policy year determines the deposit premium. An audit of actual payrolls is completed by the carrier at the end of the policy period to determine the final premium. If actual payroll is less than your estimate, a premium refund may be sent. Likewise, actual payroll higher than estimated results in an additional premium bill.

Today's business climate makes it difficult to determine who qualifies as an "employee;" the use of leased employees, subcontractors and independent contractors contributes to the confusion. Employment contracts, statute or common law usually establish employment (and employee) status. Calling a worker by a name other than employee (i.e. "subcontractor" or "independent contractor") does not overcome the facts. Additionally, how compensation is reported to the IRS (use of a 1099 Form) is not sufficient to establish that the individual is not, in fact, an employee.

Workers' compensation pays benefits to injured "employees;" any individual determined by statute or the court to be your employee is entitled to benefits. Because benefit payments are the responsibility of the insurance carrier, they are becoming very aggressive in making sure **you** pay the proper premium for the benefits **they** must provide. Insurance company auditors have traditionally allowed the use certificates of insurance to establish exemption from "employee" status. Recently, auditors have begun to disregard these certificates particularly in cases of workers' compensation "ghost" policies (a workers' compensation policy written for an unincorporated business with no employees and which does not extend coverage to the business' owner(s)).

Additionally, workers that perform the same tasks employees perform or would perform may lead the auditor to define such individuals as employees, resulting in additional premium based on the individual's compensation. These are workers you might label as "independent contractors" or "subcontractors." Depending on the number of workers in question, the premium adjustment could be substantial.

An opinion from an attorney trained in employment law is required to answer any questions about the status of a particular worker or group of workers. We as your agent appreciate the opportunity to assist you in your workers' compensation insurance program; however, we are not attorneys and are unable to provide a legal opinion as to whether a particular worker is or is not a statutory or common law employee.

Sincerely yours,

Your Independent Agent

Conclusion

Keeping other agents and clients informed allows a better system to be built. Communicating with clients up front will also avoid some heartburn in the end.

Chapter 18

A Primer on the Workers' Compensation Experience Rating Worksheet

"I've been told that my work comp experience mod is all my fault; is that true?" Over my career I've been asked this or something similar many times, as have many insurance practitioners. But the answer to this seemingly simple question isn't so simple.

Yes, the experience modification factor (Ex Mod, X-Mod, the Mod, etc.) is primarily a function of the insured's losses. But an in-depth review of the experience modification worksheet proves that at least part of the experience mod is a function of factors and/or rules promulgated by either NCCI, a Bureau or state. So, no, the insured is not totally "at fault" for the final mod.

Confused yet? Getting to the heart of the insured's experience modification factor and removing confusion requires three questions to be answered (not necessarily in the order presented).

- Why are experience modification factors developed and used?
- How is an experience modification factor developed and calculated?

- Which has greater effect on an experience modification calculation, claims frequency or claims severity?

To answer the second and third questions, this chapter breaks down the experience mod worksheet into its component parts. Each factor and rule is detailed using simple explanations and terminology. After review of this chapter, explaining the process to insureds should be easy, or at least easier.

Why Must it Be?

Beyond what the insured does (their operations), the ultimate workers' compensation premium must somehow account for how the insured manages the risks associated with what they do. One method used to measure how effectively the insured manages its employee injury risk is the experience modification factor.

Workers' compensation's base loss costs/rates are calculated considering the "average" insured within a particular class of business. Actuaries develop the concept of the "average" operational class risk by analyzing past loss experience and applying it to the probability of future losses for that class of operation. Developed loss costs/rates for each class differ from state to state to account for the loss experience differences and the expense variability among the states. (Granted, this is an over-simplified explanation of how loss costs/rates are developed; but rate development is outside the scope and purpose of this chapter.)

Use of an "average" insured rate seems reasonable, except that there is no such thing as an "average" insured or business. Each insured institutes its own philosophy and method to its business operations. Such disparate ideas and systems produce a wide range of results. "Ex mods" are a way of keeping score; of indicating whether an insured is a better-than-average risk or worse-than-average risk. In essence, the experience modification factor customizes the workers' compensation premium to match the exposure (loss experience) created or presented by an individual insured.

Actual loss experience is compared to expected loss experience (detailed later in this chapter) to develop the experience modification factor. Since the loss cost/rate is based on the "average" risk, an experience mod of 1.00 is the base line. Insureds developing a "mod" less than 1.00 (i.e. 0.80) receive a credit towards the final premium and is considered a better-than-average risk. Operations developing an experience mod higher than 1.00 (i.e. 1.15) are considered a worse-than-average risk and are penalized.

In application, the calculated "x-mod" is actually a percentage. The developed premium is multiplied by the developed mod to account for the experience of the insured.

Using the above example mods, a developed premium of $5,000 would be altered as follows

- $5,000 x 0.80 (credit mod) = $4,000
- $5,000 x 1.15 (debit mod) = $5,750

(The final estimated annual premium is developed by adding various other factors and values to the amount developed after the experience mod is applied. These values/factors may include (but only if applicable): loss constants, assigned risk charges (or ARAP), scheduled credits/debits, premium size discounts, expense constants and/or taxes.)

Not only does the experience modification factor allow the ultimate premium to conform to the exposure presented by the insured, it also allows the insured some control over its own destiny regarding the final premium. Unlike discretionary credits, the insured is entitled to the credit garnered from an experience mod less than 1.00. Additionally, the mod acts as an incentive for insureds to first avoid injuries and second to control the costs of injuries that do occur.

Only the Eligible

Not every insured qualifies for an experience modification factor. Eligibility is based on the insured's premium size. Most often the eligibility threshold is based on the total work comp premium developed over two years; and if more than two years is considered, the average of the years used must be greater than a specified amount (most commonly half the two-year total). Each state applies its own minimum premium threshold for eligibility.

Reading the Experience Rating Worksheet

Proper analysis of the results produced by the experience rating worksheet requires an understanding of the data contained in the form. The layout of the rating worksheet detracts from the flow. Example 18.1 removes the superfluous information (information not necessary to develop the final experience mod) to allow a clearer view of the calculation process.

Beginning at the top, let's work our way to the final number, the experience modification factor. Once the calculation process is detailed, this chapter will turn its focus to the variables that affect the final "mod": frequency versus severity; ERA versus Non-ERA; and how to calculate the lowest possible ex-mod for a particular insured.

From the Top

DATE. This is the effective date of the experience modification factor being calculated and is generally a function of the "Anniversary Rating Date." The Anniversary Rating Date (ARD) is the effective date of the first workers' compensation policy issued to the insured and it sets, to some extent, the effective date of the experience modification factor. The month and day of the first policy become the "anniversary rating date" that applies to each subsequent year. A specific written request is required to change the ARD.

The experience mod's effective "Date" directly affects the policy periods used by the applicable rating authority (NCCI or state rate bureau) to calculate the experience mod. These policy periods are known as the "experience period."

EXPERIENCE PERIOD. "Experience period" is NOT a term found on the worksheet; however, knowing the applicable "experience period" is required to properly analyze the worksheet. Most commonly the "experience period" is the three years ending one year prior to the experience modification factor's effective date ("Date" above). So in essence, the experience modification factor worksheet encompasses the last four policy years (48 months) but only utilizes the oldest three years (36 months) to apply towards the development of the "mod."

In Example 18.1 the effective date (Date) of the experience mod is 1/1/2020, but the "experience period" used to develop the mod ends 1/1/2019 – one year prior to the effective date. The experience period in the example is the 36 months beginning 1/1/2016 and ending 1/1/2019. Loss experience during the most current 12 months is not used for several reasons: the mod is developed several months before the policy year ends; accurate loss values may not be available; the audit cannot be completed in time; and because there may be unreported or non-compensable losses.

According to NCCI, the "experience period" can be shorter or longer than three years; as short as 12 months up to as much as 45 months. Twelve and 24 month "experience periods" are common when the insured is relatively new in business and have just become eligible for experience rating.

Some causes for the use of an experience period longer than the oldest 36 months could include the following.

- Changes in the effective rating date
- Multiple policy effective dates.
- Changes in ownership
- Interstate policy issues
- Policy periods longer than 1 year and 16 days

CODE. Indicates what the insured does as they are the classifications assignable to the insured by the authority having jurisdiction, whether it be NCCI or a state rating bureau. (See Chapter 17 for details on classification rules.) When evaluating the experience mod, these must be checked for accuracy.

ELR. The "Expected Loss Rate" is developed individually by each state based on the loss experience for the class of operation indicated by the CODE (each CODE has its own ELR). As its name suggests, this is the factor used to develop "EXPECTED LOSSES" (discussed below). The ELR is presented as a three-digit number, but in applicability it is missing a decimal point. A decimal should be inserted following the second number from the right; so in the example the ELR presented as 543 should be applied as 5.43. Likewise, the second ELR presented as 076 is applied as 0.76, and so on.

How the ELR is applied to PAYROLL to develop EXPECTED LOSSES is clarified in the applicable upcoming paragraphs.

D-RATIO. Like the ELR, the D-RATIO is specified by each individual state and is different for each class code. This ratio is used to develop the expected primary losses (EXP PRIM LOSSES) used in the final calculation of the experience mod. Also like the ELR, the D-Ratio is presented as a whole number when in applicability it is missing a decimal point. In Example 18.1, the D-Ratio shown as 10 should be applied as .10. In essence, this D-Ratio (as the term "ratio" indicates) is a percentage; the percentage is applied to the "EXPECTED LOSSES" to develop the expected primary losses (EXP PRIM LOSSES).

Chapter 18 – Experience Rating Worksheet

Example 18.1

Workers Compensation Experience Rating
ERA State

| | | | | | | **Date:** | **1/1/2020** | |
| | | | | | | **State:** | **Any with ERA** | |

EFF- Date 1/1/2016 EXP- Date 1/1/2017

Code	ELR	D-Ratio	Payroll	Exp Losses	Prim Losses	Claim Data	IJ	O/F	Act Inc Losses	Prim Losses
5645	543	10	700000	38010	3801	2007001	1	O	19000	5000
5606	076	10	100000	760	76	2007003	5	F	14500	5000
8742	020	12	110000	220	26	#8	5	F	6700	6700
8810	012	15	60000	72	11	#4	6	F	3500	3500

Policy Total   970000 (Subject Premium = 44921)   43700

EFF- Date 1/1/2017 EXP- Date 1/1/2018

Code	ELR	D-Ratio	Payroll	Exp Losses	Prim Losses	Claim Data	IJ	O/F	Act Inc Losses	Prim Losses
5645	543	10	750000	40725	4073	2008004	1	O	17000	5000
5606	076	10	105000	798	80	2008005	5	F	16500	5000
8742	020	12	115000	230	28	2008006	5	F	6700	5000
8810	012	15	62000	74	11	2008008	6	F	7500	5000
						#4	6	F	7200	7200

Policy Total   1032000 (Subject Premium = 47940)   54900

EFF-Date 1/1/2018 EXP-Date 1/1/2019

Code	ELF	D-Ratio	Payroll	Exp Losses	Prim Losses	Claim Data	IJ	O/F	Act Inc Losses	Prim Losses
5645	543	10	825000	44798	4480	2009001	2	F	9550	5000

5606	076	10	115000	874	87	2009003	5	F	3100	3100
8742	020	12	130000	260	31	2009006	5	F	5750	5000
8810	012	15	68000	82	12	#6	6	F	7200	7200

| **Policy Total** | | | **1138000** | **(Subject Premium = 56340)** | | | | | **25600** | |

(A)	(B)	(C) (D-E)	(D)	(E)	(F) (H-I)	(G)	(H)	(I)
027		**114187**	**126903**	**12716**	**54750**	**33400**	**106420**	**51670**

	(11) Primary Loss	(12) Stabilizing Value	(13) Ratable Excess	(14) Total $	(15) Exp Mod
Actual	(I) **51670**	(C)x(1-W)+(G) **116756**	(A) x (F) **14783**	(J) **183209**	
Expected	(E) **12716**	**116756**	(A) x (C) **30830**	(K) **160303**	(J)/(K) **1.14**

ELR and D-Ratio Factors. The ELR and D-Ratio factors in effect WHEN the experience mod is calculated are used for ALL years within the experience period. Thus, the ELR and D-Ratio in effect on the mod's effective date are used, not the factors in use during each of the years in the experience period.

However, there are exceptions to this rule. Delaware and Pennsylvania are those exceptions. These states apply the ELR and D-Ratio in effect during each year in the experience period. Worksheets in these two states may show different ELR and D-Ratios for each year in the experience period.

PAYROLL. Rather self-explanatory. This is the insured's audited payroll. The ELR (discussed above) is applied to PAYROLL to develop the EXPECTED LOSSES. If payrolls are incorrect, expected losses will be skewed and the entire mod calculation will be altered because many of the factors used in the final calculation are based on expected losses; and expected losses are based on accurate class codes and payroll amounts.

EXPECTED LOSSES. As the name suggests, this represents the amount of losses statistically expected per applicable classification. Notice that each class is assigned its own expected loss amount. The ELR and PAYROLL are the key factors used to calculate this amount (again, for each class) as follows:

- (PAYROLL / 100) X ELR = EXPECTED LOSSES

Remember, the ELR is missing a decimal point in front of the second numeral from the right. Using the information contained in Example 18.1, the EXPECTED LOSSES for CODE (classification code) 5645 is developed as shown here:

- (700,000 / 100) x 5.43 = 38010

As calculated, the total EXPECTED LOSSES for code 5645 are $38,010. The same calculation method is applied to each class code for every year in the experience period.

Primary vs. Excess Losses

Before moving any further into the worksheet and its calculations, the concepts of Primary and Excess losses must be detailed. As will be demonstrated more specifically later in this chapter, the total cost of the injury, to some extent, matters less than the fact that the injury occurred at all. The fact of the loss is more statistically relevant than its size because the cost of one particular injury does little to predict the amount of future losses. Remember, one purpose of the experience mod is to price for future losses.

To lessen the size of a loss' effect on the "mod" (its severity) and enhance the effect of the fact that the loss occurred (the frequency), losses are broken into two parts, "Primary" and "Excess." Primary losses are given more "weight" in the calculation as there is no weighting or credibility factor applied to these losses in the final calculation (subject to ERA in applicable states, discussed later). Excess losses are considered and applied as part of the "mod;" however excess losses are subject to a "credibility" factor lowering the amount of the excess loss that is considered in the calculation (detailed more specifically later).

What part of the loss is considered "primary" and which part is "excess?" Most often, the first $5,000 of any loss is considered to be the "primary" amount. While $5,000 is the most common, there are some state exceptions; California, for example, applies the first $7,000 as the primary amount. "Excess" losses are all amounts over $5,000 (or whatever is used as the primary amount) for one individual loss (subject to a maximum amount).

Claims exceeding the "primary" threshold must be specifically listed under CLAIM DATA and the total amount included under ACT INC LOSSES on the "mod" worksheet. Losses below the "primary" threshold can be grouped together, listing the total of all losses garnering a particular injury type (IJ). Any losses grouped together are not subject to the primary/excess concept. The total of grouped losses is included as "primary" losses.

Continuing On!

EXP PRIM LOSSES. Short for "Expected Primary Losses," this is the percentage of EXPECTED LOSSES statistically anticipated to fall under the concept of primary losses (as discussed above). Development of EXP PRIM LOSSES involves the D-RATIO and the EXPECTED LOSSES.

Once again, the D-Ratio is actually a percentage. Using the D-Ratio in Example 18.1 for class code (CODE) 5645, an EXP PRIM LOSSES amount of $3,801 is developed. In practical terms, here is the formula:

- EXPECTED LOSSES x D-RATIO = EXP PRIM LOSSES
  Or
- 38010 x 10% = $3,801

Like the EXPECTED LOSSES, this calculation is done for each class code in every year of the experience period.

CLAIM DATA. Somewhat self-explanatory; the claim number for claims exceeding a dollar amount threshold (commonly $2,000) and the number of claims in a group for those not exceeding that threshold. Information necessary to complete this section is taken from loss runs and/or unit statistical cards (unit stats).

IJ. This indicates the type, classification or severity of the injury(ies). Nine IJ codes are available.

- 1 – Death
- 2 – Permanent Total Disability
- 3 – Major Permanent Partial Disability
- 4 – Minor Permanent Partial Disability
- 5 – Temporary Total or Temporary Partial Disability
- 6 – Medical Only
- 7 – Contract Medical or Hospital Allowance

- 8 – Compromised Death – CA only
- 9 – Permanent Partial Disability

Medical only claims (IJ code 6) are of particular interest. Many states only include a portion of medical only claims in the experience mod calculation. These are called ERA states; or "Experience Rating Adjustment" states. In ERA states only 30 percent of medical only claims (including grouped medical only claims) are included in the mod calculation as part of "actual" losses. The worksheet states that the rating reflects "a decrease of 70% medical only...." Don't be confused by the use of "70%," remember that only 30% of the amount is included (and this applies to both actual total incurred and actual primary losses).

States applying ERA are: Alabama, Alaska, Arizona, Arkansas, Connecticut, DC, Florida, Georgia, Hawaii, Iowa, Idaho, Illinois, Indiana, Kansas, Kentucky, Louisiana, Maine, Maryland, Michigan, Minnesota, Mississippi, Missouri, Montana, Nebraska, Nevada, New Hampshire, New Mexico, North Carolina, Oklahoma, Rhode Island, South Carolina, South Dakota, Tennessee, Utah, Vermont, Virginia, West Virginia and Wisconsin.

O/F. Indicates the status of the claim. "O" indicates the claim is open. "F" means "final" or that the claim is closed.

ACT INC LOSSES. Actual Incurred Losses taken directly from the insured's loss information. Notice that "incurred" losses are used. Incurred losses are the total of paid and reserved losses. Only losses over a specified amount (commonly $2,000) must be specifically listed; losses below such amount can be grouped by type/severity as shown in the above IJ discussion.

Referring back to an earlier section of this chapter, remember that the fact that the loss occurred is more important than the amount of the loss. Although this more specifically relates to the development of actual primary losses (ACT PRIM LOSSES) in the next column, it also applies to Actual Incurred Losses by capping reported actual losses to a maximum amount. Each state develops its own maximum loss amount (which may be adjusted annually).

Beyond the individual loss maximum, there is a catastrophic loss maximum. This applies when more than one worker is injured in the same incident. The catastrophic loss maximum is most often two times the individual loss maximum.

What does this mean? If five workers are injured in the same incident (a wall collapses), the total loss that could/should be reported for all five men cannot exceed twice the individual loss maximum. If that's the cost for one person, so be it.

Lastly, the amount of actual incurred losses used in the form is the total of the amount of paid losses plus reserved losses on what is known as the "valuation date." The valuation date is generally six months after the end of the last policy period in the experience period.

If there is any question regarding the accuracy of the incurred loss figures for open claims, these must be discussed and resolved prior to the valuation date and calculation of the experience mod. Higher-than-necessary incurred values can affect the ultimate experience mod.

ACT PRIM LOSSES. This is the column to record the insured's Actual Primary Losses. Referring back to the earlier discussion regarding primary versus excess, only the first $5,000 (in most states) of any one single loss is included as the actual primary loss. Grouped losses are included in full as the amount represents many losses that don't exceed the individual listing limit (generally $2,000).

As part of the calculation process at the bottom of the experience rating worksheet, discussed next, actual incurred losses (ACT INC LOSSES) and actual primary losses (ACT PRIM LOSSES) applying injury code (IJ) 6 (medical only) are reduced further. The total of each "actual" amount is reduced by 70 percent; only 30 percent of medical only claims make it to the bottom of the form for calculation purposes if it's an ERA state (listed above).

Compiling the Data

Most of the information necessary to develop the experience modification factor is input and captured in the columns detailed in preceding paragraphs. However, two factors/values must be promulgated and provided by the authority calculating the "mod" (NCCI or state rating bureau):

1) the weighting (W) factor; and 2) the ballast (B) value. Both are found at the bottom of the mod worksheet and discussed in the following paragraphs. Each factor in the calculation is detailed in the following paragraphs following the same model used previously.

Box (A). This is the weighting ("W") or credibility factor supplied by the authority developing the rating worksheet (NCCI or state rating bureau). Essentially this factor represents the authority's opinion regarding the credibility of the loss data as it relates to predicting future losses. The higher the number, the more weight or credibility is given to the loss data; and likewise the lower the number the less credible the past losses are for predicting future losses.

Determination of the actual weighting factor is proprietary, but in general terms it is based directly or indirectly on the insured's premium or payroll amounts – specifically, the credibility factor is based on expected losses; and expected losses are a function of the payroll and the expected loss ratio (ELR). The smaller the risk, the less weight is given to past and expected losses – resulting in a low (A) factor; conversely, the larger the risk, the greater the weight given to past and expected losses – resulting in a higher (A) factor.

Two functions are served by the weighting factor:

1. It is applied to excess losses (expected and actual) limiting the amount of each used in the calculation; and
2. Its inverse is used to develop the stabilizing value (discussed later). The inverse is developed

by subtracting the weight factor from 1 as
follows: 1-(A) = inverse of A

This weighting/credibility factor may be presented with or
without a decimal point before the second number from the
right. Continuing to use Example 18.1, the sampled weighting
factor is "027." Some worksheets may show this number as
"0.27" or even ".27." Regardless how the value is shown, it is to
be applied as a percentage, just like the ELR and D-Ratio
discussed earlier; all three examples in this paragraph indicate
that only 27 percent of the excess losses (expected or actual) is
to be used in the calculation; and its inverse – 63 percent – is
used as part of the stabilizing value calculation.

Box (B). No one knows why this box exists; it's not used
for anything. Evidently some states use it to show the ballast
value, but most commonly this is a blank space.

Box (C): Expected Excess Losses. To develop the value
input in this box, subtract total expected primary losses (EXP
PRIM LOSSES) from total expected losses (EXPECTED
LOSSES). Total expected primary losses are found in box (E),
and total expected losses are taken from box (D).

- (D) – (E) = Expected Excess Losses (C)

The "W" factor, found in box (A), is applied to this amount
to develop the ratable excess amount applicable to expected
losses and entered in the lower box (13).

Box (D). Total Expected Losses. As was detailed
previously, expected losses are developed for each class code

for every year in the experience period. All of these developed values are added together and entered in box (D).

Box (E). Expected Primary Losses. Like box (D), box (E) is developed by adding together all the developed expected primary losses (EXP PRIM LOSSES) found in the worksheet.

Box (F). Actual Excess. Developed by subtracting the actual primary losses (box (I)) from actual incurred losses (box (H)). The "W" factor, found in box (A), is applied to this amount to develop the ratable excess amount applicable to actual losses and entered in the upper part of box (13).

Box (G). Ballast Value. The ballast value is also based on the size of the risk. The larger the risk, the higher the ballast amount. Like the "W" factor in box (A), the ballast value is promulgated by the authority developing the mod or the mod factors. As its name suggests, the ballast value is designed to avoid too great of movement away from the center/base (a mod of 1.00). It is part of the stabilizing value (found in box (12)) applied to both actual and excess values in the calculation.

Box (H). Total of Actual Incurred Losses from top of form. But keep in mind this may not be the total of the actual incurred losses (ACT INC LOSSES) presented during the experience period in states that apply ERA (experience rating adjustment) factors to medical only losses (injury code 6). In ERA states, the medical only losses are reduced by 70 percent (only 30 percent of these losses count towards the total). Thus, the amount in this box could be known as the "reduced" actual incurred losses. (Example 18.3 shows the difference between ERA and non-ERA states)

Box (I). Total of Actual Primary Losses (ACT PRIM LOSSES). Like box (H), this is the total of the actual primary losses developed in the experience period section of the worksheet. And also like box (H), the amount input in box (I) is actually the reduced total of primary losses if the risk is in an ERA state and there are medical only losses. (Also see Example 18.3.)

Compiling the Data and Calculating the Mod

All the data gathering and grouping is done, now on to the easy part, the actual calculation. Note that the "Actual" loss data is in the top boxes and the "Expected" loss data is placed in the lower boxes. At the end of this long line of date is the developed experience modification factor. Refer to Example 18.1 or another completed worksheet.

Column (11) – Primary Loss

- Top box – ACTUAL – enter the value developed in box (I) (Actual primary losses – reduced by ERA if applicable).
- Lower box – EXPECTED – input the value presented in box (E).

Column (12) – Stabilizing Value

This value has been hinted at several times throughout this chapter. The stabilizing value serves two functions: 1) sets the minimum experience mod available for any particular risk (because the total losses can NEVER be zero when a stabilizing factor is part of the calculation; and 2) it, as the name suggests, maintains balance, not allowing the experience mod to fluctuate wildly or widely. Note that the stabilizing value (12) is based on **expected** excess losses not actual losses of any kind, so there will ALWAYS be a stabilizing value.

Both the "W" factor found in box (A) and the ballast value found in box (G) are used to develop the stabilizing value. The inverse of the "W" factor is used (1-W) and the ballast amount is added. Since both the "W" factor and the ballast are affected by the size of the risk, they combine in the stabilizing value to keep it "balanced."

As is easily noted, the stabilizing value is the same for both the ACTUAL row and the EXPECTED row. The formula is:

- (C) x (1-W) + (G) = Stabilizing Value
  Or
- EXPECTED EXCESS LOSSES X (1-box (A)) + Ballast Value = Stabilizing Value

Using the inverse of the "W" value means that the more credible the authority considers the loss data to be, the lower the percentage of the Expected Excess losses (box (C)) is used to develop the stabilizing value. And the less credible the losses, the greater the amount of expected excess losses is used to calculate the stabilizing value.

As the size of the risk increases, so too does the ballast value. So even though the percentage of the expected excess value goes down as the credibility of the lass data goes up (because of the size of the risk), the effect of the lower percentage is, to some extent (not on a 1-to-1 basis), countered by the increased ballast value. Still the net result is the possibility of a lower "lowest possible" experience mod.

Column 13 – RATABLE EXCESS

This is the second place the "W" factor found in box (A) is applied. The excess losses for both actual incurred losses (box (F) and expected losses (box (C)) are multiplied by the credibility or "W" factor (a percentage value) as follows:

Top Box – ACTUAL – Box (F) x Box (A)

Lower Box – EXPECTED – Box (C) x Box (A)

Column 14 - TOTALS

Columns (11), (12) and (13) are added together to develop the total values for both the ACTUAL row (top row) and the EXPECTED row (bottom row). The total for the ACTUAL row is assigned box (J) and the EXPECTED row is box (K). Once added together, the ACTUAL total is divided by the EXPECTED total to produce the experience modification factor.

Column 15 – EXP MOD (Experience Modification Factor)

As stated above, the actual total is divided by the expected total to produce the experience modification factor. As discussed above, this indicates how well the insured manages its employee injury risk. So the final calculation looks like this:

- (J) / (K) = Experience Modification Factor

State Differences

Not all states apply the factors as presented in the above discussion. Following is the list of states that use different calculation formula; included is a calculation code key for easy reference:

Calculation Codes

AI = Actual Incurred

AP – Actual Primary

AE – Actual Excess

TEL – Total Expected Losses

EP – Expected Primary

EE – Expected Excess

WV – Weighting or

Credibility Factor

BV – Ballast Value

WMV – Weighted

Maximum Value

NCCI

$$\text{Experience Mod} = \frac{AP + (EE \times (1\text{-}WV) + BV) + (WV \times AE)}{EP + (EE \times (1\text{-}WV) + BV) + (WV \times EE)}$$

Michigan, New York, North Carolina and Wisconsin

$$\text{Experience Mod} = \frac{AP + BV + (AE \times WV) + ((1\text{-}WV) \times EE)}{EP + BV + (EE \times WV) + ((1 - WV) \times EE)}$$

- Essentially the same as NCCI's

- Each state uses the same factors, but maybe in a different
  order

Delaware and Pennsylvania

Experience Mod

=

$$\frac{(AI \times WV) + (TEL \times WMV) + TEL \times (1-WV))}{TEL}$$

- "WMV" – Unique factors developed by State. Develop factors based on premium size and expected losses
- Mod capped on either side of prior mod

Minnesota

Experience Mod

=

$$1 + \frac{((AI-TEL) \times WV) + ((AP-EP) \times (1-WV))}{TEL + BV}$$

New Jersey

Experience Mod

=

$$\frac{AEx\ WV) + (APxWMV) + (EEx(1-WV)) + (EPx(1-WMV))}{TEL}$$

- WV – Applies to Excess Losses
- WMV – Applies to Primary Losses
- TEL – Based on and calculated using Manual Premium

Texas

$$\text{Experience Mod} = \frac{AP + BV + (WV \times AE) + ((1\text{-}WV)xEE)}{TEL + BV}$$

Comparison Calculations

Frequency versus Severity

In the beginning this chapter promised to address the question of frequency versus severity and which has the greatest effect on the development of the experience modification factor. The answer has been hinted at several times throughout this chapter; frequency has a greater effect on the final "mod" than does severity.

As proof, see Example 18.2. Notice that the actual incurred loss totals are the exact same for each year of the experience period, including grouped losses and medical only losses; the difference is the number of losses crossing the primary/excess threshold in the two oldest experience period years (07-08 and 08-09).

Because of the increased frequency in losses crossing the primary/frequency threshold, the experience modification factor is 1.19 rather than the 1.14 developed in Example 18.1. This is true because of the increased number of actual primary losses coupled with the related drop in actual excess losses (which affects the mod less than primary losses).

ERA versus Non-ERA Status

Reverting back to the same loss levels presented in Example 18.1, we can compare the difference in modification factors developed in ERA versus non-ERA states. Example 18.3 vividly shows how including the entire amount of medical only claims (injury code (IJ) 6) negatively affect the final experience modification factor.

Remember, in ERA states only 30 percent of medical only losses apply in the calculation of the "mod." But in non-ERA states the entire amount of medical only claims are included in the calculation. In the example insured's case, this produces an 11 percent higher "mod": 1.25 rather than 1.14.

The effect of the ERA reduction must not be underestimated or dismissed. As stated earlier, the ERA reduction applies to both total Actual Incurred loss amounts and Actual Primary loss amounts.

Lowest Possible Experience Modification Factor

Example 18.4 shows the method for calculating the lowest possible experience mod for any insured. If there are no losses, the only factor/value in the actual row of the experience modification calculation is the Stabilizing Value. And because the Stabilizing Value is based on expected excess losses and the ballast value, there will always be a stabilizing value.

In this example, the lowest possible experience mod for the insured is 0.73.

This same process is used to show any insured what their lowest possible mod could be at any time (since the mod fluctuates based on payrolls and expected losses). Simply divide the stabilizing value found in the "Actual" loss row by the total in the "Expected" loss row found in Box K.

Experience Modification Factors

Experience mod calculations combine the insured's loss experience, the authority's opinion of the loss experience's credibility and a balancing value (the ballast value) to develop the final experience modification factor. The mod is heavily influenced by the insured's ability to manage its worker injury exposure, but factors developed by NCCI or the state rate bureau also play a part in the final factor; so the final number is not TOTALLY dependent on the insured's actions or inactions.

This chapter has detailed all parts of the experience mod worksheet. Reviewing and judging the correctness of any workers' compensation experience rating worksheet should no longer be as challenging; nor should explaining the finer points of the worksheet to an insured be a problem. Before simply accepting an experience modification factor as accurate and correct, agents, brokers, risk managers, or anyone responsible for monitoring the insured's workers' compensation program must follow this process.

1. Confirm that the class codes are correct.
2. Confirm that payrolls are correct.
3. Review reserves on Open claims BEFORE the valuation date for explanation and reasonableness.

4. Confirm, as much as possible, that the correct ELR, D-Ratio, Credibility Factor ("W" factor) and Ballast Value are correct.

5. Confirm that ERA factors have been properly applied to Actual Losses (where applicable).

6. Do a simple math calculation to confirm the reported experience mod.

Chapter 18 – Experience Rating Worksheet

Example 18.2

Workers Compensation Experience Rating
ERA State / Greater Frequency

Date: 1/1/2011

State: Any with ERA

				EFF- Date	1/1/2007		EXP- Date		1/1/2008	
Code	ELR	D-Ratio	Payroll	Exp Losses	Exp Prim Losses	Claim Data	IJ	O/F	Act Inc Losses	Act Prim Losses
5645	543	10	700000	38010	3801	2007001	1	O	7000	5000
5606	076	10	100000	760	76	2007003	5	F	14500	5000
8742	020	12	110000	220	26	2007004	5	F	12050	5000
8810	012	15	60000	72	11	#8	5	F	6700	6700
						#4	6	F	3500	3500

Policy Total   970000   **(Subject Premium = 44921)**   43750

				EFF- Date	1/1/2008		EXP- Date		1/1/2009	
Code	ELR	D-Ratio	Payroll	Exp Losses	Exp Prim Losses	Claim Data	IJ	O/F	Act Inc Losses	Act Prim Losses
5645	543	10	750000	40725	4073	2008004	1	O	11000	5000
5606	076	10	105000	798	80	2008005	5	F	14500	5000
8742	020	12	115000	230	28	2008006	5	F	6700	5000
8810	012	15	62000	74	11	2008007	5	F	8000	5000
						2008008	6	F	7500	5000
						#5	6	F	7200	7200

Policy Total   1032000   **(Subject Premium = 47940)**   54900

				EFF-Date	1/1/2009		EXP- Date		1/1/2010	
Code	ELR	D-Ratio	Payroll	Exp Losses	Exp Prim Losses	Claim Data	IJ	O/F	Act Inc Losses	Act Prim Losses
5645	543	10	825000	44798	4480	2009001	2	F	9550	5000
5606	076	10	115000	874	87	2009003	5	F	3100	3100
8742	020	12	130000	260	31	2009006	5	F	5750	5000
8810	012	15	68000	82	12	#6	6	F	7200	7200

Policy Total   1138000   **(Subject Premium = 56340)**   25600

(A) 027	(b)	(C) (D-E) 114187	(D) 126903	(E) 12716	(F)(H-I) 44800	(G) 33400	(H) 106470	(I) 61670

	(11) Primary Loss	(12) Stabilizing Value	(13) Ratable Excess	(14) Totals	(15)
	(I)	(C)x(1-W)+(G)	(A)x(F)	(J)	
Actual	61670	116756	12096	190522	Exp Mod
Expected	(E) 12716	116756	(A)x(c) 30830	(K) 160303	(J)(K) 1.19

217

Chapter 18 – Experience Rating Worksheet

Example 18.3   Workers Compensation Experience Rating
Non-ERA State

| | | | | | | | | | Date: | 1/1/2011 |

| | | | State: | | Any state with NO ERA | | | | | |
| | | | EFF- Date: | | 1/1/2007 | | | EXP-Date: | | 1/1/2008 |

Code	ELR	D-Ratio	Payroll	Exp. Losses	Exp. Prim Losses	Claim Data	IJ	O/F	Act Inc. Losses	Act Prim Losses
5645	543	10	700000	38010	3801	2007001	1	O	19000	5000
5606	076	10	100000	760	76	2007003	5	F	14500	5000
8742	020	12	110000	220	26	#8	5	F	6700	6700
8810	012	15	60000	72	11	#4	6	F	3500	3500

| **Policy Total** | | | **970000** | | **(Subject Premium= 44921)** | | | | **43700** | |

| | | | EFF- Date: | | 1/1/2008 | | | EXP- Date: | | 1/1/2009 |

Code	ELR	D-Ratio	Payroll	Exp. Losses	Exp. Prim Losses	Claim Data	IJ	O/F	Act Inc. Losses	Act Prim Losses
5645	543	10	750000	40725	4073	2008004	1	O	17000	5000
5606	076	10	105000	798	80	2008005	5	F	16500	5000
8742	020	12	115000	230	28	2008006	5	F	6700	5000
8810	012	15	62000	74	11	2008008	6	F	7500	5000
						#4	6	F	7200	7200

| **Policy Total** | | | **103200** | | **(Subject Premium= 47940)** | | | | **54900** | |

| | | | EFF- Date: | | 1/1/2009 | | | EXP- Date: | | 1/1/2010 |

Code	ELR	D-Ratio	Payroll	Exp. Losses	Exp. Prim Losses	Claim Data	IJ	O/F	Act Inc. Losses	Act Prim Losses
5645	543	10	825000	44798	4480	2009001	2	F	9550	5000
5606	076	10	115000	874	87	2009003	5	F	3100	3100
8742	020	12	130000	260	31	2009006	5	F	5750	5000
8810	012	15	68000	82	12	#6	6	F	7200	7200

| **Policy Total** | | | **1138000** | | **(Subject Premium= 56340)** | | | | **25600** | |

(A) 027	(B)	(C) (D-E) 114187	(D) 126903	(E) 12716	(F) (H-I) 56500	(G) 33400	(H) 124200	(I) 67700

	(11) Primary Loss	(12) Stabilizing Value	(13) Ratable Excess	(14) Totals	(15)
Actual	(I) 67700	(C)x(1-W)+(G) 116756	(A)x(F) 15255	(J) 199711	Exp Mod
Expected	(E) 12716	116756	(A)x(C) 30830	(K) 160303	(J)(K) 1.25

Chapter 18 – Experience Rating Worksheet

Example 18.4

Workers Compensation Experience Rating
No Losses / Lowest Possible Method

Date: 1/1/2011

State: **Any State**

EFF-Date: 1/1/2007   EXP-Date: 1/1/2008

Code	ELR	D-Ratio	Payroll	Exp. Losses	Exp. Prim Losses	Claim Data	IJ	O/F	Act Inc. Losses	Act Prim Losses
5645	543	10	700000	38010	3801					
5606	076	10	100000	760	76			No Losses		
8742	020	12	110000	220	26					
8810	012	15	60000	72	11					

Policy Total   970000   (Subject Premium= 44921)   0

EFF-Date: 1/1/2008   EXP-Date: 1/1/2009

Code	ELR	D-Ratio	Payroll	Exp. Losses	Exp. Prim Losses	Claim Data	IJ	O/F	Act Inc. Losses	Act Prim Losses
5645	543	10	750000	40725	4073					
5606	076	10	105000	798	80			No Losses		
8742	020	12	115000	220	28					
8810	012	15	62000	72	11					

Policy Total   1032000   (Subject Premium= 47940)   0

EFF-Date: 1/1/2009   EXP-Date: 1/1/2010

Code	ELR	D-Ratio	Payroll	Exp. Losses	Exp. Prim Losses	Claim Data	IJ	O/F	Act Inc. Losses	Act Prim Losses
5645	543	10	825000	44798	4480					
5606	076	10	115000	874	87			No Losses		
8742	020	12	130000	260	31					
8810	012	15	68000	82	12					

Policy Total   1138000   (Subject Premium= 56340)   0

(A) 027	(B)	(C) (D-E)	(D)	(E)	(F) (H-I)	(G)	(H)	(I)
		114187	126903	12716	0	33400	0	0

	(11) Primary Loss	(12) Stabilizing Value	(13) Ratable Excess	(14) Totals	(15)
	(I)	(C)x(1-W)+(G)	(A)x(F)	(J)	Exp Mod
Actual	0	116756	0	116756	
	(E)		(A)x(C)	(K)	(J)(K)
Expected	12716	116756	30830	160303	0.73

Appendix A

Workers' Compensation Coverage Checklist

Coverage/Risk Management Question	Y	N	Notes
Entity Type (1)			
Do any employees live outside the state of domicile or branch locations? List states. (2)			
Do any employees regularly travel out of state? Which States? (3)			
Are there any employees working from their home?			
Are home-based employee work areas inspected to assure compliance with ergonomic standards?			
Does the employer furnish any group transportation (4)?			
Do employees perform errands for the employer in their own car before or after work? (5)			
Do employees participate in employer-sponsored recreational activities (athletics, company picnics, etc.)? (5)			
Any exposure to chemicals, x-ray or radiation?			
Are Material Safety Data Sheets required and kept on site?			
Is personal protective equipment (PPE) provided and inspected regularly to confirm proper operation?			
Are employees trained in the use of PPE and required to use it at all times?			
Are any independent contractors (IC's) or subcontractors (SC's) used?			
Are current Certificates of Insurance required of all IC's and SC's? (6)			
Please provide a copy of sample contracts. Both contracts in which you AGREE to indemnify and hold harmless and those in which you			

Coverage/Risk Management Question	Y	N	Notes
TRANSFER risk to another party.			
List the states in which the insured currently conducts operations. Are they listed under 3.A.?			
What level of contractual risk transfer is allowed in each state (limited, intermediate, broad)? (7)			
Is the insured operating in any monopolistic states (ND, Ohio, Wash, or Wyo.)? (8)			
Do any employees have pre-existing medical conditions that could be compounded by a work-related injury (only applicable in states with Second Injury Funds)? (9)			
Does the employer hire temporary labor in states where they are working on a temporary basis? (10)			
Does the employer have any plans to begin operations in states not listed as a 3.A. state?			
Has the CGL policy been limited by the attachment of the CG 21 39 exclusion?			
Do employees ever travel outside the US on business?			
Do any employees work on boats on or above navigable waters? (11)			
Are there any employees with maritime exposures? (12)			
Any employees working on military bases? (12)			
Are any employees leased from an employee leasing firm? (13)			
Any employees from a PEO (co-employment)? (14)			
Does the employer ever "borrow" a worker from another employer? (13)			
Are there any other business in which the entity or the entity's owners hold a majority interest? (15)			
Are payrolls kept separated when employees are eligible for payroll splits under the interchange of labor rule?			
Are there any employees exempt from workers' compensation coverage (i.e. casual labor, domestic servants, farm laborers, etc.)? (16)			

(1) "Employee" status differs based on entity type. Corporate officers are considered employees. Sole proprietors or partners are not generally considered employees. Members/managers of LLC's may be either based on the specific statute.

(2) These states may need to be listed as 3.A. states or, at the very least, 3.C.

(3) If there are only on a temporary basis without ongoing operations, these need to be listed as 3.C. states. If on-going operations or working in such a state longer than a set amount of time, 3.A. status may be required (see particular state statute).

(4) Any injury occurring during group transportation may be considered compensable.

(5) Injury may be compensable as they may be considered "arising out of and in the course of employment." May require arbitration or a court ruling.

(6) Depending on state law, the employees of an uninsured IC's or SC's may be considered the responsibility of the Contracting party.

(7) Limited – the transferor is only protected against its vicarious liability solely for the actions of the transferee. Intermediate – the transferor is indemnified for the actions of the transferee acting alone or in connection with another party. Broad – requires the transferee to indemnify and hold harmless the transferor from all liability arising out of an incident, even if the act is committed solely by the transferor.

(8) Requires the insured to purchase WC from that state and to purchase a separate employers' liability policy.

(9) Be careful with this one. Some states with active second injury funds generally require the insured to know up front and have this information in the employees file before the SIF will pay a claim.

(10) 3.A. status will likely be necessary.

(11) If "status" and "situs" tests are satisfied, USLS&HW coverage will need to be endorsed.

(12) Specific endorsements are required for such exposures.

(13) Alternate Employer Endorsement may be necessary.

(14) Several endorsements are available based on the contract. Endorsements must be attached to both the direct employer's and the PEO's policy.

(15) Must find out if operations are combinable.

(16) Employer may want to consider providing coverage using the Voluntary Compensation Endorsement.

Appendix B

Selected Workers' Compensation Laws from all 50 States

State	WC Statute / Year Adopted	Employee Count (Non-Const./ Const.)	Members of LLC[1]	Second Injury Fund	Selected Excluded or Limited Classes of Workers (not necessarily all-inclusive)
AL	Section 25-5 / 1919	5/5	Included as employees	No (1992)	Domestic employees. Farm laborers. Casual employees, employees of municipalities having a population of less than 2,000. Leased operator or owner-operator not considered an employee.
AK	Section 23.30 / 1915	1/1	Excluded from Coverage	Yes	Non-profit corporation executive officers. Part-time baby-sitters. Residential cleaning persons. Harvest and similar part-time/transient help. Amateur event sports officials. Contract entertainers. Commercial fishers. Taxicab drivers compensated by contractual arrangement. Participants in the temporary assistance program. Professional hockey players/ coaches covered under a health care insurance plan.
AZ	23-6 / 1913	1/1	Based on tax status. Taxed as a corp. – included. Taxed as partnership – excluded.	Yes	Domestic servants working in a person's home. Independent contractor or a worker whose employment is both casual and not in the usual business of the employer. Sole proprietors with no employees.
AR	11-9 / 1939	3/2	Included as employees	No (2007)	Licensed real estate agents. Domestic servant in private home; individuals engaged in lawn or home maintenance or repair; and agricultural/farm labor. Persons

State	WC Statute / Year Adopted	Employee Count (Non-Const./ Const.)	Members of LLC[1]	Second Injury Fund	Selected Excluded or Limited Classes of Workers (not necessarily all-inclusive)
					performing services for non-profit religious, charitable or relief organizations. Any person selling or vending magazines, newspapers, etc. to the public.
CA	Division 1 and 4 / 1911	1/1	Included as employees	Yes	Domestic and residential service workers hired by the homeowner. Volunteer clerks or deputies. Persons volunteering at or for recreational camps, huts, or lodges operated by a nonprofit organization. Volunteer ski patrolmen. Non-paid volunteers for a public agency or a nonprofit organization receiving payment only for meals, transportation, lodging or incidental expenses. Any unpaid nonemployee officiating amateur sporting events sponsored by any public agency or nonprofit organization paid only a stipend for each day of service. Participants in amateur athletic events. Watchmen for nonindustrial establishments paid by subscription.
CO	Chapter 8 / 1915	1/1	Included as employees	No (1993)	Casual maintenance or repair workers performing operations for a business for a cost under $2,000 per calendar year. Domestic workers or maintenance or repair work for a private homeowner not on a full time basis. License real estate agents and brokers working on commission. Independent contractors performing specific for-hire transportation jobs. Drivers under a lease agreement with a common or contract carrier. Volunteer for a ski area operator. Persons who provide host home services as part of residential services and supports. Person that performs services for more than one employer at a race event.

Appendix B – Selected Workers' Compensation Laws

State	WC Statute / Year Adopted	Employee Count (Non-Const./ Const.)	Members of LLC[1]	Second Injury Fund	Selected Excluded or Limited Classes of Workers (not necessarily all-inclusive)
CT	Title 31 / Chap. 568 / 1913	1/1	Single-member LLC's are excluded. Multi-member LLC's are included.	No (1995)	Independent contractors. Casual employees outside business trade. Member of employer's household. Person engaged in duties involving service of the dwelling (less than 26 weeks per year).
DE	Title 19 GS 2301 / 1917	1/1	Excluded from coverage	Yes	Domestic. Farm laborers. Casual employees. Independent contractors.
DC	Division V Title 32 Chap. 15	1/1	Based on Tax status	No (1998)	Casual employees (laborers). Domestic workers in and around a private home unless the employer employed 1 or more household domestic workers for 240 hours or more during any calendar quarter in the same or the previous year. Licensed real estate salesperson or a licensed real estate broker compensated by commissions.
FL	Title XXXI Section 440/1935	4/1	Excluded except in construction codes if a member owns more than 10 % of LLC.	No (1997)	Independent contractors (IC) not in the construction industry. Real estate licensee compensated solely by commissions. Bands, orchestras, and musical and theatrical performers, including disc jockeys if IC by contract. Owner/operator of a vehicle under contract as IC. Casual laborers. Volunteers. Non-compensated workers of non-profit agencies. Exercise rider not working on a single horse. Drivers of independent taxi, limousine, or other such vehicle. Participants and officials of amateur sports events. Domestic workers. Farmers with less than five regular employees and/or 12 other seasonal agricultural workers for less than 30 days. Professional athletes.
GA	Chap. 34 Chap. 9 / 1920	3/3	Included as employees	No (2004)	Independent contractors (IC). Sports officials. Casual laborers. Domestic servants. Farm

State	WC Statute / Year Adopted	Employee Count (Non-Const./ Const.)	Members of LLC[1]	Second Injury Fund	Selected Excluded or Limited Classes of Workers (not necessarily all-inclusive)
					laborers.
HI	Chap. 386 / 1915	1/1	Included as employee; status may change	Yes	Real estate salespersons / brokers compensated solely by commissions. Volunteers of religious, charitable educational or non-profit operations. Individuals that own more than 50% of the corporation/employer. Service performed without wages by a corporate officer who owns at least 25% of the stock. Service performed by an individual solely for personal, family, or house-hold purposes provided remuneration is less than $225 during the current calendar quarter and during each completed calendar quarter of the preceding twelve-month period. Domestic workers.
ID	Title 72 / 1917	1/1	Excluded from coverage	Yes	Household domestic workers. Casual workers. Outworkers (an example would be a worker who receives mass mailing materials from the employer and assembles them at home). Family members residing in the same household. Family members of an employer's family not dwelling in the same household if a sole proprietorship provided the family member has filed a written declaration of exemption. Employment which is not carried on by the employer for the sake of pecuniary gain. Corporate officers who owns not less than 10% of the voting stock. Crop dusters under certain conditions. Associate real estate brokers and real estate sales persons compensated solely by commissions. Volunteer ski patrollers. Officials of athletic contests involving secondary schools.

Appendix B – Selected Workers' Compensation Laws

State	WC Statute / Year Adopted	Employee Count (Non-Const./ Const.)	Members of LLC[1]	Second Injury Fund	Selected Excluded or Limited Classes of Workers (not necessarily all-inclusive)
IL	Chap 820 Section 305 / 1911	1/1	Excluded from coverage unless in hazardous classification	Yes	Real estate broker compensated by commission only.
IN	Title 22 / 1915	1/1	Excluded from coverage	Yes	Casual labor. Real estate broker compensated solely by commissions. Independent contractors. Owner-operator of a motor vehicle under a written contract. Household employees. Farm and Agricultural employees (however, the term "agricultural employee" is limited to workers performing traditional types of farm labor directly related to the tending of crops and livestock. Workers injured doing other types of work in a farm setting may be covered by workers' compensation laws). Volunteers.
IA	Chap 85, 86 & 87 / 1913	1/1	Excluded from coverage	Yes	Domestic workers. Casual laborers. Agricultural workers (with provisions).
KS	Chap 44-5 / 1911	1/1	Excluded from coverage	No (1993)	Volunteers of religious and like organizations. Certain agricultural workers. Commissioned real estate agents. Employers are exempt if they have a total gross annual payroll of less than $20,000. Firefighters belong to a relief organization. Certain vehicle owner/operators.
KY	Chap 342 / 1916	1/1	Excluded from coverage	No (1996)	Employees engaged exclusively in agriculture. Domestic servants in a home with less than two full-time employees. Any person employed by homeowners for residential maintenance and repair for up to twenty (20) consecutive workdays. Workers in religious sects opposed to insurance.

State	WC Statute / Year Adopted	Employee Count (Non-Const./ Const.)	Members of LLC[1]	Second Injury Fund	Selected Excluded or Limited Classes of Workers (not necessarily all-inclusive)
LA	Title 23 / 1914	1/1	Included as employee	Yes	Domestic servants. Agricultural employees of certain unincorporated private farms with low annual payrolls. Crop duster pilots under certain conditions. Musicians and performers (conditions apply).
ME	Title 39a / 1915	1/1	Excluded from coverage	No (1992)	Agricultural or aquacultural laborers if there are six or fewer workers, or more than six meeting certain provisions. Independent contractors. Real estate broker paid solely by commissions.
MD	Title 9 / 1912	1/1	Included as employees	Yes	Casual employee. Domestic workers that earn less than $1,000 in a calendar quarter. Non-migrant farm workers working as an independent contractor. Farm workers if the farmer has less than three employees or an annual payroll of less than $15,000. Home maintenance worker if hired for less than 30 days. Owner/operator hired as independent contractor (IC). Real estate broker paid solely by commission. Some volunteer workers in political subdivisions.
MA	Chap 152 / 1911	1/1	Excluded from coverage	Yes	Professional athletes whose contracts provide for the payment of wages during the period of any employment-related disability. Real estate salesperson compensated solely by commissions. Direct seller not in a retail establishment. Taxicab operator leasing the vehicle from the taxicab company. Casual employee. Domestic workers.
MI	Chap 418 / 1912	1/1 (if specific provisions are met, employer can have up to 3	Included as employee	Yes	Agricultural employees under specific circumstances (based on number and length of employment). Domestic workers if employed less than full time. Real estate agent or broker

State	WC Statute / Year Adopted	Employee Count (Non-Const./ Const.)	Members of LLC[(1)]	Second Injury Fund	Selected Excluded or Limited Classes of Workers (not necessarily all-inclusive)
		employees).			provided at least 75 percent of income is commissions and the contract states they are not an employee. Independent contractor.
MN	Chap 176 / 1913	1/1	Excluded from coverage if there are 10 or fewer m embers and less than 22,880 hours of payroll in the preceding calendar year provided that manager owns at least a 25% membership interest in the LLC.	No (1995)	Some executive officers (subject to percentage of ownership, number of shareholders and payroll hour limitations). Family farm employees paying less than $8,000 in the preceding year; operations with $300,000 in total liability insurance and $5,000 in farm laborer medical insurance may pay up to the statewide average annual wage before WC coverage is required. Executive officers of a family farm corporation. Casual employees. Household workers (includes a domestic, repairer, groundskeepers or maintenance worker at a private household earning less than $1,000 during a quarter of the year). Veteran's organization officers and members attending meetings and conventions. Nonprofit associations with a total annual payroll of less than $1,000. Workers covered under the Domestic Volunteer Service Act of 1973 (Vista volunteers, foster grandparents). Independent contractors.
MS	Title 71 / 1948	5/5	Included as employee but can reject under certain conditions. If so, does not count toward the 5.	Yes	Domestic laborers. Farm laborers. Employees of non-profit fraternal, charitable, religious or cultural organizations are not covered. Independent contractors (special protection is given to employees of subcontractors).
MO	Chap 287 / 1926	5/1	Included as employee	Yes	Farm laborers. Domestic workers. Occasional home maintenance workers. Certain real estate agents. Volunteers at

State	WC Statute / Year Adopted	Employee Count (Non-Const./ Const.)	Members of LLC[1]	Second Injury Fund	Selected Excluded or Limited Classes of Workers (not necessarily all-inclusive)
					tax-exempt organizations. Sports officials for schools. Owner-operator of certain motor vehicles.
MT	39-71 / 1915	1/1	Excluded from coverage	Yes	Independent contractor. Household or domestic employees. Most volunteers. Trustee of rural fire department.
NE	Chap 48 / 1913	1/1	Excluded from coverage	No (1997)	Agricultural workers if working less than 13 calendar weeks in a year. Casual employees. Executive officers owning more than 25% of the common stock. Executive officers of non-profits paid less than $1,000. Certain owner-operators and lessor-operators.
NV	Chap 616 a-d and Chap 617 / 1913	1/1	Included as employee	Yes	Casual laborers whose work does not last more than 20 days. Theatrical/stage performers. Musicians not working more than 2 days. Most domestic, farm, diary, agricultural or horticultural workers. Voluntary ski patrolmen. Sports officials at amateur events. Clergyman, rabbi or lay reader in the service of a church, or any person occupying a similar position with respect to any other religion. Real estate agents paid by commission. Direct sellers (not retail) and commissioned workers.
NH	RSA 281-A / 1911	1/1	Excluded from coverage if less than 3 members; included as employees if over 4 members.	Yes	LLC's with 3 or less members and no other employees. Seller or qualified real estate broker or agent solely compensated by commissions. Real estate appraiser paid on a fee-for-service basis. Direct seller. Independent contractor.
NJ	34-15 / 1911	1/1	Excluded from coverage	Yes	Casual employees. Domestic workers.

Appendix B – Selected Workers' Compensation Laws

State	WC Statute / Year Adopted	Employee Count (Non-Const./ Const.)	Members of LLC[(1)]	Second Injury Fund	Selected Excluded or Limited Classes of Workers (not necessarily all-inclusive)
NM	Chap 52 and 59 / 1917	3/1	Included as employee	No (1996)	Casual labor (except in contractor classifications). Real estate sales person paid by commission. Farm and ranch workers (with exceptions).
NY	WKC Articles 1-11 / 1913	1/1	Excluded from coverage	No (2007)	Domestic workers working less than 40 hours per week. Farm workers paid less than $1,200 per year. Volunteers for non-profit organizations. Clergy and other members of religious orders. Participants and officials of amateur athletics. Teachers for non-profit religious, charitable or educational institution. Spouse and minor children of a farmer. People doing yard work and other chores around houses and non-profit institutions (coverage required if minor uses power driven machinery). Certain real estate salespeople, media representatives and insurance agents/brokers who sign a contract that they are independent contractors. Independent contractors
NC	NCGS 97 / 1929	3/3 (1 if there is radiation present)	Excluded from coverage	Yes	Domestic, farm and casual employees provided there are less than 10 regularly employed. Volunteer ski patrol. Newspaper resellers. Sellers of agricultural products working on commission.
ND	Chap 65 / 1919	1/1	Excluded from coverage	Yes	Independent contractor. Casual laborers. Employer's spouse or child (under 21). Real estate salesperson paid by commission (based on contract provisions). Member of a board of directors. Newspaper sellers acting as independent contractors. Customer agricultural operations and agricultural operations lasting less than 30 days.

Appendix B – Selected Workers' Compensation Laws

State	WC Statute / Year Adopted	Employee Count (Non-Const./ Const.)	Members of LLC[1]	Second Injury Fund	Selected Excluded or Limited Classes of Workers (not necessarily all-inclusive)
OH	Chap 4121 and 4123 / 1911	1/1	Excluded from coverage if chooses to be taxed as a partnership. Included as an employee if taxed as a corporation.	Yes	A duly ordained, commissioned, or licensed minister or assistant or associate minister of a church in the exercise of ministry. Officers of a family farm corporation. An incorporated individual. An individual who otherwise is an employee of an employer but who signs the waiver and affidavit. Domestic employees paid less than $160 in a calendar quarter.
OK	Title 85 / 1915	1/1	Excluded if own more than 10% of stock	No (2000)	Five or less total employees related to the employer by blood or marriage. Domestic servants and casual laborers of a private residence provided total payroll is less than $10,000. Agriculture or horticulture workers provided prior calendar year's gross annual payroll was less than $100,000 for such workers. Real estate sales associate or broker, paid on a commission basis. Youth sports league workers.
OR	Chap 656 / 1913	1/1	Excluded from coverage	Yes	Domestic workers. Casual laborers. Garden, maintenance or repair workers at residence hired by homeowner. Firefighters and police in municipalities having a population greater than 200,000 with a disability and retirement program. Amateur athletes. Some volunteers. Ski patrol volunteers. A person older than 18 contracting as an independent contractor with a publisher to sell papers, etc. Amateur sports officials. Language translators provided by another entity.
PA	Title 77 / 1915	1/1	Excluded from coverage Section 104 of the Act, 77 P.S.	Yes	Casual workers. Agricultural laborers earning under $1200 per person per calendar year AND no one agricultural laborer works 30 days or more per calendar year. Domestic workers. Been granted exemption due to

Appendix B – Selected Workers' Compensation Laws

State	WC Statute / Year Adopted	Employee Count (Non-Const./ Const.)	Members of LLC[1]	Second Injury Fund	Selected Excluded or Limited Classes of Workers (not necessarily all-inclusive)
			Section 22		religious beliefs. Licensed real estate agents paid by commissions only.
RI	Chap 28: 29-41 / 1912	1/1	Included as employee	No (1998)	Domestic workers. Non-hazardous agricultural workers unless there are employed more than 25 workers for more than 13 weeks. Licensed real estate brokers or salespersons, or licensed or certified real estate appraisers provided substantially all remuneration is commission or fee-based.
SC	Title 42 / 1935	4/4 (1 if ionizing radiation is present)	Excluded from coverage	No (2012)	Casual workers. Agricultural employees, and employers who had a total annual payroll during the previous year of less than $3,000, regardless of the number of workers employed. Independent sellers of agricultural products. Real estate agents paid by commission. Certain owner-operators or lease-operators of motor vehicles.
SD	Title 62 and 58-20 / 1917	1/1	Included as employee	No (1999)	Domestic servants, unless working for more than 20 hours in any calendar week and for more than 6 weeks in any 13-week period. Farm or agricultural labor. Independent contractors. Real estate agents and owner-operators of trucks who are certified as independent contractors. Officers of non-profits.
TN	Title 50, Chap 6 / 1919	5/1	Excluded from coverage	Yes	Leased operator or owner operator contracted to a common carrier. Domestic workers. Farm and agricultural laborers. Volunteer ski patrol.
TX	Labor Code Title 5 / 1913	Elective / 1	Law is silent, probably Included as	Yes	Work comp is elective except certain construction classes are required to carry coverage.

State	WC Statute / Year Adopted	Employee Count (Non-Const./ Const.)	Members of LLC[(1)]	Second Injury Fund	Selected Excluded or Limited Classes of Workers (not necessarily all-inclusive)
			employee		
UT	Title 34A / Chap 2 / 1917	1/1	Included as employee	No (1994)	Agricultural laborers provided payroll is less than $50,000 (agricultural operations with payroll between $8,00-$50,000 have the option of either workers' compensation coverage or liability coverage). Casual labor. Domestic workers. Real estate brokers.
VT	Title 21, Chap 9 / 1915	1/1	Included as employee	No (1999)	Casual employees. Person involved in amateur sports. Agricultural or farm employment w/ less than $10,000 in total annual payroll. Resident relatives. Domestic workers. Real estate broker paid by commission only.
VA	65.2 / 1918	3/3	Excluded from coverage	Yes	Independent contractor (with exceptions). Some elected officials. Real estate salesperson paid by commissions. Independent taxicab or limo driver. Casual worker. Domestic worker. Farm and horticultural workers unless there are 3 or more regularly employed farm/horticultural workers. Non-compensated employees. Amateur sporting event officials.
WA	RCW 51 / 1911	1/1	Included as employee	Yes	Independent contractor. Domestic workers provided there are less than two working 40 hours per week. Gardening, maintenance or repair for a private homeowner. Child under 18 employed by parents in agricultural activities. Jockeys while participating in or preparing for certain races. Newspaper carrier.
WV	Chap 23 / 1913	1/1	Included as employee	No (2003)	Domestic workers. Agricultural workers provided there are 5 or fewer full time employees. Casual employers with fewer than 3 employees. Churches.

Appendix B – Selected Workers' Compensation Laws

State	WC Statute / Year Adopted	Employee Count (Non-Const./Const.)	Members of LLC[1]	Second Injury Fund	Selected Excluded or Limited Classes of Workers (not necessarily all-inclusive)
					Those involved in professional sports. Volunteer rescue personnel under certain conditions.
WI	Chap 102 / 1911	3/3	Excluded from coverage	Yes	Farm laborers (unless employ 6 or more for 20 days in a calendar year). Domestic workers. Independent contractors performing operations unrelated to the employer. Volunteer at a tax exempt organization.
WY	27-14 / 1915	1/1	Excluded from coverage	Yes	Casual labor. Independent contractor. Spouse or dependent of employer in the same household. Professional athlete (with exceptions). Domestic worker. Private duty nurse engaged by a private party. Volunteers. Owner-operator of vehicle under contract-of-hire. An individual providing child day care or babysitting services, whose wages are subsidized or paid in whole or in party by the Wyoming department of family services.

(1) Most states that exclude members of an LLC from the law allow the members to elect coverage if desired. Likewise, if members of an LLC are included as an employee, most states allow the members to exclude themselves from coverage if they so desire.

Appendix C
NCCI's Workers' Compensation Policy

WORKERS COMPENSATION AND EMPLOYERS LIABILITY INSURANCE POLICY

WC 00 00 00 C
(Ed. 1-15)

WORKERS COMPENSATION AND EMPLOYERS LIABLITY INSURANCE POLICY

In return for the payment of the premium and subject to all terms of this policy, we agree with you as follows:

GENERAL SECTION

A. The Policy

This policy includes at its effective date the Information Page and all endorsements and schedules listed there. It is a contract of insurance between you (the employer named in Item 1 of the Information Page) and us (the insurer named on the Information Page). The only agreements relating to this insurance are stated in this policy. The terms of this policy may not be changed or waived except by endorsement issued by us to be part of this policy.

B. Who is Insured

You are insured if you are an employer named in Item 1 of the Information Page. If that employer is a partnership, and if you are one of its partners, you are insured, but only in your capacity as an employer of the partnership's employees.

C. Workers Compensation Law

PART ONE
WORKERS COMPENSATION INSURANCE

A. How This Insurance Applies

This workers compensation insurance applies to bodily injury by accident or bodily injury by disease. Bodily injury includes resulting death.

1. Bodily injury by accident must occur during the policy period.

2. Bodily injury by disease must be caused or aggravated by the conditions of your employment. The employee's last day of last exposure to the conditions causing or aggravating such bodily injury by disease must occur during the policy period.

B. We Will Pay

We will pay promptly when due the benefits required of you by the workers compensation law.

C. We Will Defend

We have the right and duty to defend at our expense any claim, proceeding or suit against you for benefits payable by this

WORKERS COMPENSATION AND EMPLOYERS LIABILITY INSURANCE POLICY

WC 00 00 00 C
(Ed. 1-15)

Workers Compensation Law means the workers or workmen's compensation law and occupational disease law of each state or territory named in Item 3.A. of the Information Page. It includes any amendments to that law which are in effect during the policy period. It does not include any federal workers or workmen's compensation law, any federal occupational disease law or the provisions of any law that provide nonoccupational disability benefits.

D. State

State means any state of the United States of America, and the District of Columbia.

E. Locations

This policy covers all of your workplaces listed in Items 1 or 4 of the Information Page; and it covers all other workplaces in Item 3.A. states unless you have other insurance or are self-insured for such workplaces.

insurance. We have the right to investigate and settle these claims, proceedings or suits.

We have no duty to defend a claim, proceeding or suit that is not covered by this insurance.

D. We Will Also Pay

We will also pay these costs, in addition to other amounts payable under this insurance, as part of any claim, proceeding or suit we defend:

1. reasonable expenses incurred at our request, but not loss of earnings;
2. premiums for bonds to release attachments and for appeal bonds in bond amounts up to the amount payable under this insurance;
3. litigation costs taxed against you;
4. interest on judgment as required by law until we offer the amount due under this insurance; and
5. expenses we incur.

E. Other Insurance

We will not pay more than our share of benefits and costs covered by this insurance and other insurance or self-insurance. Subject to any limits of liability that may apply, all shares will be equal until the loss is paid. If any insurance or self-insurance is exhausted, the shares of all remaining insurance will be equal until the loss is paid.

F. Payments You Must Make

You are responsible for any payments in excess of the benefits regularly provided by the workers compensation law including those required because:

1. of your serious and willful misconduct;

WORKERS COMPENSATION AND EMPLOYERS LIABILITY INSURANCE POLICY

WC 00 00 00 C
(Ed. 1-15)

2. you knowingly employ an employee in violation of law;

3. you fail to comply with a health or safety law or regulation; or

4. you discharge, coerce or otherwise discriminate against any employee in violation of the workers compensation law.

If we make any payments in excess of the benefits regularly provided by the workers compensation law on your behalf, you will reimburse us promptly.

WORKERS COMPENSATION AND EMPLOYERS LIABILITY INSURANCE POLICY

WC 00 00 00 C

(Ed. 1-15)

G. Recovery From Others

We have your rights, and the rights of persons entitled to the benefits of this insurance, to recover our payments from anyone liable for the injury. You will do everything necessary to protect those rights for us and to help us enforce them.

H. Statutory Provisions

These statements apply where they are required by law.

1. As between an injured worker and us, we have notice of the injury when you have notice.

2. Your default or the bankruptcy or insolvency of you or your estate will not relieve us of our duties under this insurance after an injury occurs.

3. We are directly and primarily liable to any person entitled to the benefits payable by this insurance. Those persons may enforce our duties; so may an agency authorized by law. Enforcement may be against us or against you and us.

4. Jurisdiction over you is jurisdiction over us for purposes of the workers compensation law. We are bound by decisions against you under that law, subject to the provisions of this policy that are not in conflict with that law.

5. This insurance conforms to the parts of the workers compensation law that apply to:
a) benefits payable by this insurance;
b) special taxes, payments into security or other special funds, and assessments payable to us under that law.

6. Terms of this insurance that conflict with the workers compensation law are changed by this statement to conform to that law. Nothing in these paragraphs relieves you of your duties under this policy.

bodily injury that arises out of and in the

PART TWO
EMPLOYERS LIABILITY INSURANCE

A. How This Insurance Applies

This employers liability insurance applies to bodily injury by accident or bodily injury by disease. Bodily injury includes resulting death.

1. The bodily injury must arise out of and in the course of the injured employee's employment by you.

2. The employment must be necessary or incidental to your work in a state or territory listed in Item 3.A. of the Information Page.

3. Bodily injury by accident must occur during the policy period.

4. Bodily injury by disease must be caused or aggravated by the conditions of your employment. The employee's last day of last exposure to the conditions causing or aggravating such bodily injury by disease must occur during the policy period.

5. If you are sued, the original suit and any related legal actions for damages for bodily injury by accident or by disease must be brought in the United State of American, its territories or possessions, or Canada.

B. We Will Pay

We will pay all sums you legally must pay as damages because of bodily injury to your employees, provided the bodily injury is covered by this Employers Liability Insurance.

The damages we will pay, where recovery is permitted by law, include damages:

1. For which you are liable to a third party by reason of a claim or suit against you by that third party to recover the damages claimed against such third party as a result of injury to your employee;

2. For care and loss of services; and

3. For consequential bodily injury to a spouse, child, parent, brother or sister of the injured employee; provided that these damages are the direct consequence of

WORKERS COMPENSATION AND EMPLOYERS LIABILITY INSURANCE POLICY

WC 00 00 00 C
(Ed. 1-15)

course of the injured employee's employment by you; and

4. Because of bodily injury to your employee that arises out of and in the course of employment, claimed against you in a capacity other than as employer.

C. Exclusions

This insurance does not cover:

1. Liability assumed under a contract. This exclusion does not apply to a warranty that your work will be done in a workmanlike manner;

2. Punitive or exemplary damages because of bodily injury to an employee employed in violation of law;

3. Bodily injury to an employee while employed in violation of law with your actual knowledge or the actual knowledge of any of your executive officers;

4. Any obligation imposed by a workers compensation, occupational disease, unemployment compensation, or disability benefits law, or any similar law;

5. Bodily injury intentionally caused or aggravated by you;

6. Bodily injury occurring outside the United States of America, its territories or possessions, and Canada. This exclusion does not apply to bodily injury to a citizen or resident of the United States of America or Canada who is temporarily outside these countries;

7. Damages arising out of coercion, criticism, demotion, evaluation, reassignment, discipline, defamation, harassment, humiliation, discrimination against or termination of any employee, or any personnel practices, policies, acts or omissions;

8. Bodily injury to any person in work subject to the Longshore and Harbor Workers' Compensation Act (33 U.S.C. Sections 901 et seq.), the Nonappropriated Fund Instrumentalities Act (5 U.S.C. Sections 8171 et seq.), the Outer

E. We Will Also Pay

Continental Shelf Lands Act (43 U.S.C. Sections 1331 et seq.), the Defense Base Act (42 U.S.C. Sections 1651-1654), the Federal Mine Safety and Health Act (30 U.S.C. Sections 801 et seq. and 901-944), any other federal workers or workmen's compensation law or other federal occupational disease law, or any amendments to these laws;

9. Bodily injury to any person in work subject to the Federal Employers' Liability Act (45 U.S.C. Sections 51 et seq.), any other federal laws obligating an employer to pay damages to an employee due to bodily injury arising out of or in the course of employment, or any amendments to those laws;

10. Bodily injury to a master or member of the crew of any vessel, and does not cover punitive damages related to your duty or obligation to provide transportation, wages, maintenance, and cure under any applicable maritime law;

11. Fines or penalties imposed for violation of federal or state law; and

12. Damages payable under the Migrant and Seasonal Agricultural Worker Protection Act (29 U.S.C. Sections 1801 et seq.) and under any other federal law awarding damages for violation of those laws or regulations issued thereunder, and any amendments to those laws.

D. We Will Defend

We have the right to and duty to defend, at our expense, any claim, proceeding or suit against you for damages payable by this insurance. We have the right to investigate and settle these claims, proceedings and suits.

We have no duty to defend a claim, proceeding or suit that is not covered by this insurance. We have no duty to defend or continue defending after we have paid our applicable limit of liability under this insurance.

WORKERS COMPENSATION AND EMPLOYERS LIABILITY INSURANCE POLICY

WC 00 00 00 C

(Ed. 1-15)

We will also pay these costs, in addition to other amounts payable under this insurance, as part of any claim, proceeding, or suit we defend:
1. Reasonable expenses incurred at our request, but not loss of earnings;
2. Premiums for bonds to release attachments and for appeal bonds in bond amounts up to the limit of our liability under this insurance;
3. Litigation costs taxed against you;
4. Interest on a judgment as required by law until we offer the amount due under this insurance; and
5. Expenses we incur.

F. **Other Insurance**
We will not pay more than our share of damages and costs covered by this insurance and other insurance or self-insurance. Subject to any limits of liability that apply, all shares will be equal until the loss is paid. If any insurance or self-insurance is exhausted, the shares of all remaining insurance and self-insurance will be equal until the loss is paid.

G. **Limits of Liability**
Our liability to pay for damages is limited. Our limits of liability are shown in Item 3.B. of the Information Page. They apply as explained below.
1. Bodily Injury by Accident. The limit shown for "bodily injury by accident – each accident" is the most we will pay for all damages covered by this insurance because of bodily injury to one or more employees in any one accident.
A disease is not bodily injury by accident unless it results directly from bodily injury by accident.
2. Bodily Injury by Disease. The limit shown for "bodily injury by disease – policy limit" is the most we will pay for all damages covered by this insurance and arising out of bodily injury by disease, will apply as though that state were listed

regardless of the number of employees who sustain bodily injury by disease. The limit shown for "bodily injury by disease – each employee" is the most we will pay for all damages because of bodily injury by disease to any one employee.
Bodily injury by disease does not include disease that results directly from a bodily injury by accident.
3. We will not pay any claims for damages after we have paid the applicable limit of our liability under this insurance.

H. **Recovery from Others**
We have your rights to recover our payment from anyone liable for an injury covered by this insurance. You will do everything necessary to protect those rights for us and to help us enforce them.

I. **Actions Against Us**
There will be no right of action against us under this insurance unless:
1. You have complied with all the terms of this policy; and
2. The amount you owe has been determined with our consent or by actual trial and final judgment.
This insurance does not give anyone the right to add us as a defendant in an action against you to determine your liability. The bankruptcy or insolvency of you or your estate will not relieve us of our obligations under this Part.

**PART THREE
OTHER STATES INSURANCE**

A. **How This Insurance Applies**
1. This other states insurance applies only if one or more states are shown in Item 3.C. of the Information Page.
2. If you begin work in any one of those states after the effective date of this policy and are not insured or are not self-insured for such work, all provisions of the policy

WORKERS COMPENSATION AND EMPLOYERS LIABILITY INSURANCE POLICY

WC 00 00 00 C

(Ed. 1-15)

in Item 3.A. of the Information Page.

3. We will reimburse you for the benefits required by the workers compensation law of that state if we are not permitted to pay the benefits directly to persons entitled to them.

4. If you have work on the effective date of this policy in any state not listed in Item 3.A. of the Information Page, coverage will not be afforded for that state unless we are notified within 30 days.

B. **Notice**

Tell us at once if you begin work in any state listed in Item 3.C. of the Information Page.

PART FOUR
YOUR DUTIES IF INJURY OCCURS

Tell us at once if injury occurs that may be covered by this policy. Your other duties are listed here.

1. Provide for immediate medical and other services required by the workers compensation law.

2. Give us or our agent the names and addresses of the injured persons and of witnesses, and other information we may need.

3. Promptly give us all notices, demands and legal papers related to the injury, claim, proceeding or suit.

4. Cooperate with us and assist us, as we may request, in the investigation, settlement or defense of any claim, proceeding or suit.

5. Do nothing after any injury occurs that would interfere with our right to recover from others.

6. Do not voluntarily make payments, assume obligations or incur expenses, except at your own cost.

D. **Premium Payments**

PART FIVE
PREMIUM

A. **Our Manuals**

All premium for this policy will be determined by our manuals of rules, rates, rating plans and classifications. We may change our manuals and apply the changes to this policy if authorized by law or a governmental agency regulating this insurance.

B. **Classifications**

Item 4 of the Information Page shows the rate and premium basis for certain business or work classifications. These classifications were assigned based on an estimate of the exposures you would have during the policy period. If your actual exposures are not properly described by those classifications, we will assign proper classifications, rates and premium basis by endorsement to this policy.

C. **Remuneration**

Premium for each work classification is determined by multiplying a rate times a premium basis. Remuneration is the most common premium basis. This premium basis includes payroll and all other remuneration paid or payable during the policy period for the services of:

1. all your officers and employees engaged in work covered by this policy; and

2. all other persons engaged in work that could make us liable under Part One (Workers Compensation Insurance) of this policy. If you do not have payroll records for these persons, the contract price for their services and materials may be used as the premium basis. This paragraph 2 will not apply if you give us proof that the employers of these persons lawfully secured their workers compensation obligations.

WORKERS COMPENSATION AND EMPLOYERS LIABILITY INSURANCE POLICY

WC 00 00 00 C

(Ed. 1-15)

You will pay all premium when due. You will pay the premium even if part or all of a workers compensation law is not valid.

E. Final Premium

The premium shown in the Information Page, schedules, and endorsements is an estimate. The final premium will be determined after this policy ends by using the actual, not the estimated, premium basis and the proper classifications and rates that lawfully apply to the business and work covered by this policy. If the final premium is more than the premium you paid to us, you must pay us the balance. If it is less, we will refund the balance to you. The final premium will not be less than the highest minimum premium for the classifications covered by this policy.

If this policy is cancelled, final premium will be determined in the following way unless our manuals provide otherwise:

1. If we cancel, final premium will be calculated pro rata based on the time this policy was in force. Final premium will not be less than the pro rata share of the minimum premium.

2. If you cancel, final premium will be more than pro rata. It will be based on the time this policy was in force and increased by our short-rate cancelation table and procedure. Final premium will not be less than the minimum premium.

F. Records

You will keep records of information needed to compute premium. You will provide us with copies of those records when we ask for them.

G. Audit

You will let us examine and audit all your records that relate to this policy. These records include ledgers, journals, registers, vouchers, contracts, tax reports, payroll and disbursement records, and programs

D. Cancelation

for storing and retrieving data. We may conduct the audits during regular business hours during the policy period and within three years after the policy period ends. Information developed by audit will be used to determine final premium. Insurance rate service organizations have the same rights we have under this provision.

PART SIX
CONDITIONS

A. Inspection

We have the right, but are not obliged to inspect your workplaces at any time. Our inspections are not safety inspections. They relate only to the insurability of the workplaces and the premiums to be charged. We may give you reports on the conditions we find. We may also recommend changes. While they may help reduce losses, we do not undertake to perform the duty of any person to provide for the health or safety of your employees or the public. We do not warrant that your workplaces are safe or healthful or that they comply with laws, regulations, codes or standards. Insurance rate service organizations have the same rights we have under this provision.

B. Long Term Policy

If the policy period is longer than one year and sixteen days, all provisions of this policy will apply as though a new policy were issued on each annual anniversary that this policy is in force.

C. Transfer of Your Rights and Duties

Your rights or duties under this policy may not be transferred without our written consent. If you die and we receive notice within thirty days after your death, we will cover your legal representative as insured.

WORKERS COMPENSATION AND EMPLOYERS LIABILITY INSURANCE POLICY

WC 00 00 00 C

(Ed. 1-15)

1. You may cancel this policy. You must mail or deliver advance written notice to us stating when the cancelation is to take effect.

2. We may cancel this policy. We must mail or deliver to you not less than ten days advance written notice stating when the cancelation is to take effect. Mailing that notice to you at your mailing address shown in Item 1 of the Information Page will be sufficient to prove notice.

3. The policy period will end on the day and hour stated in the cancelation notice.

4. Any of these provisions that conflict with a law that controls the cancelation of the insurance in this policy is changed by this statement to comply with the law.

E. **Sole Representative**

The insured first named in Item 1 of the Information Page will act on behalf of all insureds to change this policy, receive return premium, and give or receive notice of cancelation.

Appendix D

Workers' Compensation Endorsement Listing and Description

Endorsement Name	Form No.	Description / Notes
Workers Compensation and Employers Liability Policy	WC 00 00 00 C	NCCI policy form
Workers Compensation and Employers Liability Policy Information Page & Extensions	WC 00 00 01 A	Declaration Page with standard information.
Defense Base Act Coverage Endorsement	WC 00 01 01 A	Extends USL&HW-level benefits to civilian employees or civilian contractors working on military bases outside the continental US (includes Alaska & Hawaii). Removes the Defense Base Act exclusion (within exclusion "8") from the employers' liability coverage wording.
Federal Coal Mine Health and Safety Act Coverage Endorsement	WC 00 01 02 B	Extends WC and EL benefits to employees as per Federal limits and guidelines to employees that contract "Black Lung."
Federal Employers' Liability Act Coverage Endorsement	WC 00 01 04 A	Workers' Compensation coverage does not apply in any state listed in the FELA Coverage Endorsement. Coverage is subject to Federal guidelines and requirements to garner protection. Exclusion "9" is removed. Employers' Liability coverage is extended to the states and up to the limits specified by the endorsement. No each employee "bodily injury by disease" limit, only a disease aggregate limit.
Longshoremen's and Harbor Workers' Compensation Act Coverage Endorsement	WC 00 01 06 A	Extends / raises statutory WC benefits to comply with the benefits required by the USL&HW Act as specified by the Federal government. Rates may be higher to account for the increased benefits. Removes the USL&HW exclusion (within exclusion "8") from the employers' liability coverage wording.

Appendix D – WC Endorsement Listing and Description

Endorsement Name	Form No.	Description / Notes
Nonappropriated Fund Instrumentalities Act Coverage Endorsement	WC 00 01 08 A	Extends USL&HW-level benefits to civilian employees working on military bases within the continental US removes the Nonappropriated Funds exclusion (within exclusion "8") from the employers' liability coverage wording.
Outer Continental Shelf Lands Act Coverage Endorsement	WC 00 01 09 C	Extends USL&HW-level benefits to workers on fixed structures located outside of territorial waters but within Outer Continental Shelf exclusion (within exclusion "8") from the employers' liability coverage wording.
Migrant and Seasonal Agricultural Worker Protection Act Coverage Endorsement	WC 00 01 11	Extends coverage to work subject to the Migrant and Seasonal Agricultural Worker Protection Act. Part Two Exclusion 12 does not apply to work subject to the act.
Notification Endorsement of Pending Law Change to Terrorism Risk Insurance Program Reauthorization Act of 2015	WC 00 01 15	This endorsement notifies policyholders that TRIPRA may expire before the end of their policy term.
Maritime Coverage Endorsement	WC 00 02 01 B	Extends benefits to the limits required by maritime or admiralty law (Jones Act or DHSA included). Removes exclusion "10." Adds two exclusions: no coverage if P&I coverage and no coverage for transportation, maintenance and cure unless a premium is paid.
Voluntary Compensation Maritime Coverage Endorsement	WC 00 02 03	WC 00 02 01A must first be attached. Extends WC coverage to masters and members of a crew when such is not required by law. Extends employers' liability coverage to masters and members of the crew when not required by law to provide coverage.
Alternate Employer Endorsement	WC 00 03 01 A	Designed to extend coverage when employees are considered the "borrowed servants" of a special employer. It is attached to the direct employer's policy, naming the special employer thus extending protection from the employer's policy to the putative employer.
Designated Workplaces Exclusion Endorsement	WC 00 03 02	Use to exclude designated work places but only when proper and allowable in the law.
Employers Liability Coverage Endorsement	WC 00 03 03 C	Extends employers' liability coverage to monopolistic states (ND, Ohio, Wash. And Wyo.).

247

Appendix D – WC Endorsement Listing and Description

Endorsement Name	Form No.	Description / Notes
Insurance Company as Insured Endorsement	WC 00 03 04	Limits coverage to the insurance carrier's employees only.
Joint Venture as Insured Endorsement	WC 00 03 05	Limits coverage exclusively to employee's of the joint venture. Policy does not provide coverage for employees of the members of the joint venture.
Medical Benefits Exclusion Endorsement	WC 00 03 06	Makes the insured solely responsible for paying medical benefits. Used mainly by self-insurers.
Partners, Officers and Other Exclusion Endorsement	WC 00 03 08	Used for individuals considered an employee by law (varies by state) yet chooses to exclude themselves from the law and the benefits available from WC coverage. Exclusion can be accomplished by name or by position.
Rural Utilities Service Endorsement	WC 00 03 09 B	Assures compliance with RUS guidelines.
Sole Proprietors, Partners, Officers and Other Coverage Endorsements	WC 00 03 10	Extends employees status and benefits to persons normally excluded from coverage (varies by state)
Voluntary Compensation and Employers Liability Coverage Endorsement	WC 00 03 11 A	Signifies that an employer has voluntarily chosen to provide workers' compensation coverage and benefits to those not required, by state law, to be covered.
Voluntary Compensation and Employers Liability Coverage for Residence Employees Endorsement	WC 00 03 12A	Same as WC 00 03 11 A except limited to domestic workers.
Waiver of our Right to Recover from Others Endorsement	WC 00 03 13	Waives the insurance carrier's subrogation rights against the scheduled entity.
Workers Compensation and Employers Liability Coverage for Residence Employees Endorsement	WC 00 03 14 A	This endorsement is used when the employer is statutorily required to insure domestic workers (varies by state). The endorsement is designed to be used with homeowners' policies, personal liability policies or similar personal policies.
Domestic and Agricultural Workers Exclusion Endorsement	WC 00 03 15	Used to exclude coverage for domestic and agricultural workers in states where such exclusion is allowed. Applies when the employers employs other workers subject to the law but wants to exclude coverage for domestics and agricultural workers.

Endorsement Name	Form No.	Description / Notes
Professional Employer Organization Extension Endorsement	WC 00 03 20 B	This endorsement extends workers' compensation and employers' liability benefits exclusively from the PEO. Attached to the PEO's policy. This extension only applies to employees leased to the client(s) listed on the schedule.
Professional Employer Organization Exclusion Endorsement	WC 00 03 21	Attached to the PEO's workers' compensation policy to exclude coverage for employees leased to the client(s) scheduled in the form. This endorsement is used when the client leases employees on an "other-than-short-term" basis and such client is charged with providing the workers' compensation benefits.
Professional Employer Organization Client Exclusion Endorsement	WC 00 03 22	Attached to the employer's/ client's workers' compensation policy to exclude the extension of workers' compensation benefits to employees leased on a long-term basis from the labor contractor (PEO) scheduled in the policy. Only used when the PEO is responsible for providing coverage.
Multiple Coordinated Policy Endorsement	WC 00 03 23	This endorsement extends benefits to the leased employees rather than having to depend on a staffing firm to extend coverage.
Residual Market Multiple Company Endorsement	WC 00 03 25	Attached to employer's policies insured in the residual market with operations in multiple states and the operations in the other states is insured by a separate subsidiary of the insurer.
Residual Market Limited Other States Insurance Endorsement	WC 00 03 26A	Extends "Other States" benefits on a limited basis when WC coverage is placed in a residential market.
Aircraft Premium Endorsement	WC 00 04 01 A	Indicates the additional premium required under WC code 7421 under passenger seat code 9108.
Anniversary Rating Date Endorsement	WC 00 04 02	Used if the anniversary rating date (related to the experience mod) is different than the policy effective dates. May result from mid-term cancellation and re-write or other cause.
Experience Rating Modification Factor Endorsement	WC 00 04 03	Allows the insurance carrier to change the experience mod mid-term.
Pending Rate Change Endorsement	WC 00 04 04	Allows the insurance carrier to change rates mid-term.

Appendix D – WC Endorsement Listing and Description

Endorsement Name	Form No.	Description / Notes
Policy Period Endorsement	WC 00 04 05	Used when the policy period is longer than 1 year and 16 days and does not consist of complete 12 month periods. Might be used to get to a common effective date.
Premium Discount Endorsement	WC 00 04 06 A	Shows the calculation for the premium discount.
Rate Change Endorsement	WC 00 04 07	Like the WC 04 04, only the rates have already been approved and will be effective on the specified date.
Longshore and Harbor Workers' Compensation Act Rate Change Endorsement	WC 00 04 08	Like the WC 04 04, only the rates have already been approved and will be effected on the specified date. Applies only to USL&HW coverage.
Contingent Experience Rating Modification Factor Endorsement	WC 00 04 12	A contingent mod was used to calculate the premium. A new premium calculation will be completed once the final mod is calculated.
90-Day Reporting Requirement – Notification of Change in Ownership Endorsement	WC 00 04 14 A	Requires the Insured to report changes in ownership within 90 days (ERM-14).
Assigned Risk Adjustment Program Endorsement assigned	WC 00 04 15 A	Attached to insured's in risk (or other such residual programs) that are also subject to additional charges (i.e. ARAP charges).
Assigned Risk Loss Sensitive Rating Plan Notification Endorsement	WC 00 04 17 A	Notification that an insured in assigned risk plans that reaches a specified premium level may be subject to a retrospective rating plan, regardless of desire.
Assigned Risk Mandatory Loss Sensitive Rating Plan Endorsement	WC 00 04 18 C	Like WC 00 04 17 A, except the insured knows up front and this endorsement supplies the rating factors.
Premium Due Date Endorsement	WC 00 04 19	Simply requires the insured to pay when billed.
Domestic Terrorism, Earthquakes, and Catastrophic Industrial Accidents Premium Endorsement	WC 00 04 21 D	Notification to the insured that there is additional premium to cover the risk of domestic terrorism or a catastrophic accident.
Foreign Terrorism Premium Endorsement	WC 00 04 22 B	Allows the insured to charge for and define a foreign terrorist act.

Appendix D – WC Endorsement Listing and Description

Endorsement Name	Form No.	Description / Notes
Audit Noncompliance Charge Endorsement	WC 00 04 24	Provides a method to add an audit noncompliance charge when the insured does not allow the audit to take place.
Experience Rating Modification Factor Revision Endorsement	WC 00 04 25	Provides that the experience rating modification factor may change and if it does, the policy will be endorsed with the new factor.
Retrospective Premium Endorsement One Year Plan	WC 00 05 03 D	Attached to the policy of insured's whose coverage is written on a retrospectively rate (loss sensitive) plan. Endorsement defines the plan and gives the rating factors.
Retrospective Premium Endorsement Three Year Plan	WC 00 05 04 D	Like WC 00 05 03 D, except for three-year retro plans.
Retrospective Premium Endorsement Wrap-Up Construction Project	WC 00 05 05 D	Like WC 00 05 03 D, except intended to apply towards long-term construction projects.
Retrospective Premium Endorsement Aviation Exclusion	WC 00 05 08	Used when the aviation exposure is not subject to the retrospective rating plan.
Retrospective Premium Endorsement Changes	WC 00 05 09 A	Used when there are changes in the retrospective rating factors or their inapplicability in certain states.
Retrospective Premium Endorsement Nonratable Catastrophe Element or Surcharge	WC 00 05 10	Used when a retrospectively rated policy covers a non-ratable catastrophe element or surcharge. Aircraft operations and explosives and ammunition manufacturing classifications are examples.
Retrospective Premium Endorsement Short Form	WC 00 05 11	Used when the insured has more than one retrospectively rated policy subject to the same rating options.
Retrospective Premium Endorsement One Year Plan – Multiple Lines	WC 00 05 12 D	Defines retrospective rating, the rating elements and how the premium is calculated. Allows other lines of coverage such as GL and Auto to be included in the calculation of the final premium using the same factors.
Retrospective Premium Endorsement Three Year Plan – Multiple Lines	WC 00 05 13 D	Same as WC 00 05 12D, except applies to three year policies.
Retrospective Premium Endorsement Long-Term	WC 00 05 14 D	Same as WC 00 05 12 D, except applies to long-

Appendix D – WC Endorsement Listing and Description

Endorsement Name	Form No.	Description / Notes
Construction Project – Multiple Lines		term construction projects.
Retrospective Premium Endorsement Flexibility Options	WC 00 05 15 A	Indicates in which states the incurred losses have been changed to include loss adjustment expenses.
Retrospective Rating Plan Premium Endorsement Large Risk Alternative Rating Option (LRARO)	WC 00 05 16	This endorsement is attached when a retrospective rating plan is used.
Benefits Deductible Endorsement	WC 00 06 03	If the insured operates in a state what allows a WC deductible and to which benefits the deductible apply (medical and indemnity, medical only or indemnity only).

Appendix E
First Report of Injury Requirements for all 50 States

State	Statute	Form Used	Injuries that must be reported to Regulatory Authorities (All injuries must be reported to carrier)	Time Limit to Report
AL	25-5-4	WCC Form 2	All reported injuries	Within 15 days of occurrence of injuries
AK	AS 23.30.095(c).	Form 07-6101	All reported injuries	Immediately, but in no case later than 10 days after you have knowledge that your employee has been injured, or claims to have been injured or become ill. If beyond 10 days, subject to penalty equal to 20% of compensation due.
AZ	23-908	Form ICA 04-0101 (Rev. 7/01)	All reported injuries	Within 10 days after receiving notification of a work related injury or disease. Fatalities within 24 hours.
AR	11-9-529	Form 1A-1	Those involving either more than 7 days of lost time or indemnity of payments	Within 10 days.
CA	Chapter 7 Article 1 Section 14005	DWC-1 and DLSR 5020	Any physical or mental injury caused by the job which results in lost time beyond the date of the incident or requires medical treatment beyond first aid, or death.	Must be submitted in writing within 5 days of any prescribed occupational injury or illness. Injuries must be reported immediately by phone to the nearest California OSHA office.
CO	8-43-101	WC1	All injuries or occupational disease	Within 10 days after notice or knowledge of the injury

State	Statute	Form Used	Injuries that must be reported to Regulatory Authorities (All injuries must be reported to carrier)	Time Limit to Report
			which result in lost time from work in excess of 3 shifts or calendar days, or in permanent physical impairment, or fatality.	or disease. Fatalities must be reported to your insurance carrier immediately.
CT	CGS 31-316	WCC-15	Occurrence, injury or disease resulting in incapacity form work of one day or more	Report is to be filed within 1 week of notice.
DE	19-2313	DOC. No. 60-07-01-90-10-04	All injuries	Within 10 days.
FL	69L-3.004	DWC-1	All cases except first aid cases	Within 7 days of notice
GA	34-9-12	WC-1	Any injury requiring medical or surgical treatment or causing absence from work for more than 7 days.	In writing within 10 days.
HI	386	WC-1	Every work injury to an employee causing absence for one day or more or which requires medical services other than first aid treatment must be reported.	Within 7 days of the injury.
ID	72-602	IA-1 (02/98)	If a work-related injury or illness results in one-day lost work time or requires medical treatment.	As soon as practicable, but not later than ten (10) days after the occurrence.
IL	Section 6 (b) of WC Act	IA-1 or IC-45	All injuries resulting in loss of more than 3 scheduled workdays or results in death.	Must report within 3 days. Fatalities must be reported within 2 days.
IN	IC 22-3-4-13	SF-34401	Injuries that result in death or employees absence from work for more than 1 day.	Within 7 days of occurrence or knowledge (whichever is later).
IA	86.11	IAIABC	Any occupational injury or	Electronically within four

State	Statute	Form Used	Injuries that must be reported to Regulatory Authorities (All injuries must be reported to carrier)	Time Limit to Report
		FORM 1.2 (12/98)	illness which temporarily disables an employee for more than three days or which results in permanent total disability, permanent partial disability, or death.	business days of specified event. Within eight hours each accident or health hazard that results in one or more fatalities or hospitalization of three or more employees.
KS	K.S.A. 44-557(a)	K-WC 1101-A (Rev. 2-06)	Any accident or claimed or alleged accident resulting in whole or partial incapacity that continues beyond the "day, turn, or shift which such injuries are sustained" as the result of accident.	Within 28 days of the receipt of knowledge of such incapacity.
KY	KRS 342.038	IA-1	All reported injuries	Immediately, but no more than 3 working days of notice.
LA	RS 23:1306 and 1310	LWC-WC-1007	Death or more than seven days of disability. Or If there is notice of a disputed claim.	Within 10 days of injury.
ME	30-A M.R. S.A. Sec. 303	WCB-1	Injuries resulting in the loss of a day's work.	Carrier must be notified within 7 days.
MD	9-707	IA-1	Death or injury resulting in more than 3 days of disability. Occupational disease.	Within 10 days for injury. Immediately for disease.
MA	MGI Chapter 152	Form 101	Employee is injured, or alleges injury and is unable to earn full wages for 5 or more calendar days.	Within 7 business days from the 5th day of disability.
MI	Rule 408.31	Form WC-100	Injury or disease resulting in death or disability extending beyond seven days or other "specific" loss.	Within 7 calendar days of receiving notice.
MN	176.231	MN FR01 (02/06)	Death or serious injury arising from employment. Or if the employee cannot	Within 24 hours if death or serious injury. Within three days if employee cannot

Appendix E – First Report of Injury Requirements

State	Statute	Form Used	Injuries that must be reported to Regulatory Authorities (All injuries must be reported to carrier)	Time Limit to Report
			work for a period of more than three days.	work for more than three days. Must be entered into SEMA4 and sent within three calendar days.
MS	71-3-65 and 67	IA-1	Injuries or illnesses resulting in death, permanent disability, serious head or facial disfigurement or disability lasting longer than five days.	Within 10 days.
MO	287.380.1	WC-1-EDI	Any accident resulting in injury.	Within 10 days after knowledge of injury.
MT	39-71-307	ERD-991	All injuries or illnesses.	Within six days of notice.
NE	Rule 29	NWCC Form 1	All injuries or illnesses.	Within 10 days after knowledge of injury.
NV	NRS 616C.015	C-1	All injuries or illnesses.	As soon as practicable.
NH	281-A:53	Form 8WC	Any occupational disease or injury. Injury resulting in disability of four or more days requires a separate form (13WCA).	As soon as possible, but not later than 5 days after the employee learns of such an injury. Form 13WCA must be filed within 7 days.
NJ	R.S. 34:15-96	IA-1	All injuries reported to carrier.	Insurance CARRIER reports all accidents within 3 weeks of learning of the accident.
NM	52-1-58	NM WCA FORM E1.2	All work related injuries or illnesses resulting in death or more than seven days of lost work.	Within 10 days of injury or illness giving rise to reportable incident.
NY	Sect. 110 WC Law	C-2	All injuries causing a loss of time from regular duties of one day beyond the working day or shift.	Within 10 days after the accident occurs.
NC	NCGS 97-92	Form 19	Any accident causing more than 1 days absence from work or more than $2,000	Within 5 days after knowledge of accident.

Appendix E – First Report of Injury Requirements

State	Statute	Form Used	Injuries that must be reported to Regulatory Authorities (All injuries must be reported to carrier)	Time Limit to Report
			in medical cost.	
ND	65-05-01.4	SFN 2828 (05/2007)	Any injury or illness.	Filed with Workforce Safety & Insurance (WSI)
OH	4123-28 4123-3-03	On-Line FROI-1	Injuries and occupational diseases resulting in seven days or more of total disability or death. All injuries must be reported to the State. Ohio is a Monopolistic State Fund and must be notified of all injuries.	Reported specified injury or diagnosis of occupational disease to the bureau of workers' compensation within one week of acquiring knowledge of such injury or death or the diagnosis or death from the occupational disease.
OK	Section 24.1	Form 2	Accidental injury which 1) results in lost time beyond the shift; 2) requires medical attention away from the work site; 3) is fatal.	Within 10 days.
OR	656.262	440-801	Any injury that may be compensable must be reported.	Reports to insurance carrier within five days. Fatalities must be reported within 8 hours and overnight hospitalization within 24 hours to state OSHA.
PA	Section 438 of WC Act	LIBC-344	Any injury resulting in the loss of a full turn or shift of work.	As soon as possible.
RI	28-32-1 (Rules)	DWC-01	Any work-related injury requiring any medical treatment or if the employee loses full wages for at least 3 days. The employer must also report any work-related death.	Within 10 days of knowledge of the injury OR within 48 hours of death.
SC	42-19-10	Form 12A	Only injuries requiring more than $500 in medical cost or which results in permanency.	Within 10 days.
SD	SDCL 62-6-2	DOL-LM-101	Employers are required to complete an Employer's First Report of Injury form	The employer has 7 days excluding Sundays and holidays to submit this

State	Statute	Form Used	Injuries that must be reported to Regulatory Authorities (All injuries must be reported to carrier)	Time Limit to Report
			and submit it to their worker's compensation insurance carrier.	form.
TN	0800-2-14-.03 (1)	LB-0021	All reported injuries.	Within 1 working day of knowledge of injury.
TX	8308-5.05 Texas	TWCC-1	All injuries resulting in the absence from work beyond the date of the accident, or any occupational disease.	Must file the loss with the Insurance WC Act Carrier within 8 days after the employees absence from work or notice of occupational disease. Do not send to the State unless specifically requested.
UT	34A-2 and 34 A-3	Form 122	Any injury that results in medical treatment by a physician, loss of consciousness, loss of work, or transfer to another job.	Within 7 days of incident. Within 12 hours if (Form 1-A1) injury results in fatality; disabling, serious, or significant injury; or occupational disease incident. "Serious injury" includes: amputation, fractures of major bones, and hospitalization for medical treatment.
VT	Sec. 8. 21 V.S.A. § 640 (e)	Form 1	All injuries and illnesses. Employer must report but can elect to pay medical bills that are less than $750.	Electronically within 72 hours of accident.
VA	65.2.900	VWC Form #3	1) lost time exceeding 7 days; 2) medical expenses exceed $100; 3) results in death; 4) permanent disability or disfigurement	When notified of injury.
WA	Claims are filed through the injured worker's healthcare provider. In 2008, the state began a two-year pilot program that will allow the injured working to file the claim through the employer or the healthcare provider. Under this pilot program, the employer has two days to file an incident report once the report is completed. Visit http://www.lni.wa.gov/IPUB/242-378-000.pdf for more information. Currently, employees have up to one year to give the employer notice of a work-related injury. WCC C1 form is used to report injury. Whenever an employer has notice or knowledge of an injury or occupational disease sustained by any worker in his or her employment who has received treatment from a physician or a licensed advanced registered nurse practitioner, has been hospitalized, disabled from work or has died as the apparent result of such injury or			

Appendix E – First Report of Injury Requirements

State	Statute	Form Used	Injuries that must be reported to Regulatory Authorities (All injuries must be reported to carrier)	Time Limit to Report
			occupational disease, the employer shall immediately report the same... (RCW 51.28.025)	
WA DC	32-1532	FORM NO. 8 DCWC	All injuries.	Within 10 days of DC injury or knowledge.
WV	23-4-1 b	WC-3	All reported injuries.	Within 5 days of receipt of notification of the employee's injury, or within 5 days after the employer has been notified by the Commissioner that a claim for benefits has been filed on account of an injury.
WI	DWD Administrative Code 80.02(2)(a)	WKC-12-E	Employers must report all injury claims to their insurance carrier within 7 days of the incident.	Insurance carriers must report injuries which result in four days or more lost time from work to the Worker's Compensation Division within 24 hours of the incident.
WY	Chapter 4 of Wyoming Rules Section 3 and 27-14-502	INJRPT	All injuries. The injured worker is required by the statute to report the occurrence and general nature of the injury to the employer as soon as practical within 72 hours after the injury becomes apparent.	The employer must file a report of injury within 10 days after the date on which the employer is notified of the injury.

Appendix F

Glossary

Abandonment of Employment

Engaging in an activity clearly not intended for the advancement of the employer nor directed by or anticipated by the employer. Includes any activity in direct contradiction to the rules, requests or expectations of the employer.

"Arising out of..."

A casual connection between the furtherance of the employer's business and the injury. If the employer benefits in some way from the activity, then the injury or illness suffered in the pursuit of that activity is considered to "arise out of" the employment.

Assumption of Risk

A defense against charges of negligence barring or severely limiting an individual's recover under the tort of negligence. The defendant must prove that 1) the plaintiff was reasonably aware of and appreciated the danger involved; 2) the plaintiff voluntarily exposed himself to the danger; and 3) the assumed danger was the proximate cause of the injury or damage.

Broad Transfer

Provides the greatest scope of contractual risk transfer and requires the transferee to indemnify and hold harmless the transferor from all liability arising out of an incident, even if the act is committed solely by the transferor. This may qualify as an exculpatory contract and is illegal in some jurisdictions because the wording is considered "unconscionable."

Casual Labor

Work that is not in the usual course of trade, business, occupation or profession of the employer (contracting party). The contractors hired are not performing duties that would normally be done by an employee; they are doing work outside the normal operational requirements. Essentially, a casual laborer is one that does not directly promote or advance the employers business or operation.

Coming and Going Rule

Injury suffered traveling to or home from work or even while going to and returning from lunch is generally not compensable. The logic behind the rule is that the employee is not furthering the employer's interest or serving the business' needs.

Contract of Hire

"Contract of hire" states approach the issue of extraterritorial jurisdiction and when to name a 3.A. state from the employment contract standpoint. The state of hire is essentially the deciding factor. The vast majority of states statutorily subscribe to this approach; however court decisions often hearken back to the "significant contact" test.

Contractual Risk Transfer

A formal agreement between two parties whereby one agrees to indemnify and hold another party harmless for specified acts. Such transfer encompasses both Risk Financing (planning for the cost of a loss) and Risk Control (developing means to avoid or lessen the cost of a loss). The intended goal of contractual risk transfer is to place the financial burden of a loss on the party best able to control and prevent the loss. There are three parties to and three levels of contractual risk transfer.

Contributory Negligence

Doctrine of defense stating that if the injured person was even partially culpable in causing or aggravating his own injury he is barred from any recovery from the other party. This is an absolute defense.

De Facto Employee

De facto means "in fact or in reality." Employers may call a de facto employee an independent contractor when they are "in fact" an employee. The degree of control often influences the worker's classification as a true independent contractor or a de facto employee.

De Jure Employee

De jure means "by right, according to the law." A de jure employee is an employee created by an act of law. In most states, injured employees of an uninsured subcontractor become the responsibility of the general contractor; they become the "de jure employees" of the general contractor by action of workers' compensation law.

Doctrinal Employer- Employee Relationship (Special Employer)

1) The employee made a contract of hire, express or implied, with the special employer? In essence, has the direct employer volunteered or directed the employee to work for the special employer and has the employee agreed to such assignment; 2) The work being done essentially that of the special employer; and 3) The special employer has the right to control the details of the work.

Employee

A person hired to perform certain services or tasks for particular wages or salary under the control of another (the employer); or a worker hired to perform a specific job <u>usual and customary</u> to the employer's business operation in exchange for money or other remuneration.

Exculpatory

An agreement altering tort and contract law. The root term "exculpate" means to hold another blameless for their future actions. Commonly used in waivers to protect one party against injury suits from another party while participating in activities that may prove inherently dangerous. Exculpatory agreements generally cannot be used to avoid statutory requirements, common law duties, criminal penalties or negligence in tort (duties owed to the public cannot be contracted away). If there is unequal bargaining strength between the parties to the contract, an exculpatory clause may be considered unconscionable and thus unenforceable. These rules vary by jurisdiction.

Fellow Servant Rule

Defense against employer negligence asserting that an employee's injury was caused by a fellow employee not by the acts of the employer. If proven, negligence was not asserted against the employer and recovery could be severely limited or barred.

General Contractor

An individual or entity with whom the principal/owner directly contracts to perform specified jobs. Some or all of the enumerated tasks are subsequently contracted to other entities (subcontractors) for performance. Three parties are required before any entity is considered a general contractor: a principal, an independent contractor, and a subcontractor hired by the independent contractor. The independent contractor's status changes to that of a general contractor when any part of the work is subcontracted to another entity.

General Exclusion Classifications

These are the opposite of "standard exception" classes. General exclusion class activities are completely unexpected and are not considered part of the analogy of the governing classification of most operations. Employees engaged in general exclusion activities require separation to allow the insurer to garner the, usually, higher premium for the increased exposure.

Operations and activities falling within the general exclusion classification are: 1) Employees working in aircraft operations; 2) Employees performing new construction or alterations; 3) Stevedoring employees; 4) Sawmill operation employees; and 5) Employees working in an employer-owned daycare.

General Inclusion Classifications

Some activities are considered to be an integral part of the business' operations thus the payroll of the individuals engaged in these activities is included in the governing classification. These activities include: 1) Employees that work in a restaurant, cafeteria or commissary run by the business for use by the employees (this does not apply to such establishments at construction sites); 2) Employees manufacturing containers such as boxes, bags, can or cartons for the employer's use in shipping its own products; 3) Staff working in hospitals or medical facilities operated by the employer for use by the employees; 4) Maintenance or repair shop employees; and 5) Printing or lithography employees engaged in printing for the employer's own products.

Ghost Policy   A "ghost" policy is a workers' compensation policy written for an unincorporated business with no employees and which does not extend coverage to the business' owner(s).

Indemnitor   The party called on to respond financially. This can include the "Transferee" or an insurance company.

Independent Contractor   An entity with whom a principal/owner directly contracts to perform a certain task or tasks. Independent contractors are generally engaged to perform operations not within the usual trade or business of the principal and such tasks are contract specific. All work required of the contract is performed by the independent contractor and employees.

Interchange of Labor Rule   The interchange of labor rule is an exception to the governing classification rule. Applicability of this rule varies by state; some states only allow its use in the construction, erection or stevedoring classes of business while other states permit the interchange of labor rule to apply to any type of business operation. Interchange of labor rules allow a single employee's payroll to be split between or among several class codes that may be present within the operations. Certain requirements must be met before this rule can be applied.

Intermediate Transfer   The transferee agrees to accept the financial consequences of occurrences caused in whole *or in part* by its negligence. This includes if the transferor or another entity contributes to the loss in some way.

"In the course..." A function of the timing and location of the injury or illness. The implication is that the injury must occur during operations for the employer, or "during employment," and at the employer's location or a location mandated or reasonably expected by the employer.

Legal Person (a.k.a. Juridical Person) A legal fiction, a "person" created by statute and "born" with the filing of articles of incorporation (or organization). These legal persons are given the right to own property, sue and be sued. Corporations are legal persons. Several states consider LLC's a legal person making the managers and members employees.

Limited Liability Company (LLC) An LLC is a hybrid legal entity combining the advantages (mostly tax-based) of a partnership and the liability protection offered by a corporation. Members are simply the owners of the LLC and may or may not participate in the day-to-day management of the company. Members involved in the management maintain a dual role as a member and a manager.

Limited Transfer The narrowest level of contractual risk transfer. The transferee only accepts the financial consequences of loss resulting from his/its sole negligence. If the transferor or another party contributes to the loss, the transferee is not financially responsible for that part of the loss. Essentially, the transferor is only protected for its vicarious liability arising out of the actions of the transferee.

Majority Interest Majority interest is created when the same

(Combinability)	person or group of person(s) combine to own more than 50 percent of an entity and can be created in many ways: 1) An entity or persons (as detailed above) owns the majority of the voting stock of another entity; or both entities share a majority of the same owners (if there is no voting stock). Generally these are natural persons that own multiple entities. 2) If neither of the above applies, majority interest is created if a majority of the board is common between two or among several entities. 3) Participation of each general partner in the profits of the partnership (limited partners are excluded). 4) When ownership interest is held by an entity as a fiduciary (excludes a debtor in possession, a trustee under an irrevocable trust or a franchisor).
Monopolistic States	Employers can purchase a workers' compensation policy only from the state. Only four monopolistic states are still in operation: North Dakota, Ohio, Washington and Wyoming. Employers' liability coverage is not offered by these states and this coverage must be procured by alternate means.
Natural Person	A flesh and blood human being. In workers' compensation the employer is a natural person(s) in sole proprietorships and partnerships. Managers and members of an LLC are viewed as natural persons in a majority of states making these natural persons the employers.
Occupational Disease	Illness directly attributable to work conditions and exposures; such injury or illness must arise out of and in the course and scope of

employment. To be considered "occupational" and therefore compensable, the disease must arise out of or be caused by conditions peculiar to the work. Medical opinion leading to the conclusion that an illness is work-related is not necessarily based on the disease but on the facts surrounding the patient's sickness.

Permanent Partial Disability

The employee has suffered an injury from which he will never recover, but one that will not prevent him from returning to some type of work. Amputation of a finger or leg, the loss of an eye or ear are examples of this injury classification.

Permanent Total Disability

Recovery is not predicted; the employee is not expected to ever be able to return to work. Full paralysis, total blindness and total loss of hearing are examples of such an injury.

Putative Employer

The special employer rather than the direct employer. Status as the "employer of record" at such a specific time is "put" upon the individual or entity based on several factors, the most obvious is the amount of control the person/entity has over the worker.

Respondeat Superior:

Latin for "let the master answer."

"Scope of employment..."

Analyzes the motivations of the employee, the employer's direction and control over the actions of the employee; and the employer's foresee ability of the activities of the employee. Employee actions which ultimately lead to an accident or injury must be motivated, in whole or in part, by the "desire" to further the interests of the employer. Motivation or desire can be out of fear that failure to perform will result in the loss of a job, or from a more altruistic desire to do well for the employer. The basis for the motivation or desire is irrelevant; it is the fact that the motivation exists that leads to compensability. Further, the actions must, to some extent, be at the presumed direction of the employer or potentially foreseen by the employer.

Significant Contact Test This test is applied when making jurisdictional decisions – which state benefits can the employee access. Significant contact tests base these jurisdictional decisions around the employee. Three primary tests/questions work to determine which states need to be scheduled as primary, 3.A. states. These questions are: 1) Where does the employee live? 2) Where does the employee primarily work? And 3) In what state was the contract of hire made? If a "preponderance of contact" evidences a state not listed as a 3.A. state, there may be a gap in protection.

Situs The first test before an employee can be considered a longshoreman or harbor worker. Situs requires that the employment be on, above or below navigable waters and adjoining areas. However, working around or over water does not in itself qualify an individual for the benefits prescribed by USL&HW Act law. To qualify for such coverage requires satisfying the "status" test.

Standard Exception Some duties/activities are considered so common to most business and/or such duties

Classifications

may be so far outside the operational activities of the business that employees engaged in these activities are considered exceptions to the governing classification rules. Payroll for these "standard exception" classes of employees is subtracted from the governing classification and assigned to the applicable standard exception code and rated separately from the governing class. The standard exception classes include: 1) Clerical Employees – Class Code 8810; 2) Clerical Telecommuter – Class Code 8871; 3) Drafting Employees – Class Code 8810; 4) Salespersons – C ass Code 8742; and 5) Drivers – Class Code 7380.

Standard exception classifications are not necessarily limited to these five class codes; some states utilize state-specific class codes that are also eligible for assignment as a standard exception.

Status

To be considered a longshoreman or harbor worker requires that the employment involve the loading and unloading of ships; or the maintenance, repair or dismantling of ships.

Subrogation

Individuals or entities suffering injury and/or damage due to the negligence of another person or entity have the right to recover costs and expenses from the at-fault party. If, however, the injured party chooses to seek reimbursement from its own insurance carrier, the rights of the injured party are transferred to the insurance carrier. Subrogation rights for the insurance carrier flow from the right of its insured to recover payment. If the insured does not have the right to recover payment, neither does its insurance carrier. Contractual risk transfer provisions often limit the rights of one party to recover from another party for injury or damage. When the right of the insured to recover is waived via a contract, lost is the insurer's right to subrogate.

Temporary Partial Disability   A full recovery from the injury is expected, but for a period of time the employee is completely unable to work due to the injury. These types of injuries might require bed rest or hospitalization while the employee recovers.

Temporary Total Disability   A full recovery from the injury is expected, but for a period of time the employee is completely unable to work due to the injury. These types of injuries might require bed rest or hospitalization while the employee recovers.

Transferee   The party accepting the risk in a contractual risk transfer agreement. This can include the general contractor and subcontractors. Other common terms include indemnitor and promisor.

Transferor   The party from who risk is being transferred in a contractual risk transfer agreement. This may include the owner, the project management firm, and/or the general contractor. Other common terms for the transferor include indemnitee and promisee.

Unconscionable   A contract or contract provision that is unreasonable due to the unequal bargaining strength of the parties, or the result of undue influence or unfair tactics.

Author Biography

Christopher J. Boggs is the Executive Director Risk Management and Education for the Independent Insurance Agents and Brokers of America. He joined the insurance industry in 1990 and is a self-proclaimed insurance geek with a true passion for the insurance profession and a desire for continual learning.

During his career, Boggs has authored hundreds of insurance and risk management-related articles on a wide range of topics as diverse as Credit Default Swaps, the MCS-90, and enterprise risk management.

Boggs has written and published five insurance and risk management books, including these best-sellers.

- *"The Insurance Professional's Practical Guide to Workers' Compensation: From History through Audit – Second Edition;"*
- *"Business Income Insurance Demystified: The Simplified Guide to Time Element Coverages – Second Edition;"*
- *"Property and Casualty Insurance Concepts Simplified: The Ultimate 'How to' Insurance Guide for Agents, Brokers, Underwriters and Adjusters;"*

A graduate of Liberty University with a bachelor's degree in Journalism, Boggs has continually pursued career-related education, obtaining nine professional insurance designations:

the Chartered Property Casualty Underwriter (**CPCU**), Associate in Risk Management (**ARM**), Associate in Loss Control Management (**ALCM**), Legal Principles Claims Management (**LPCS**), Accredited Advisor in Insurance (**AAI**), Associate in Premium Auditing (**APA**), Certified Workers' Compensation Advisor (**CWCA**), Construction Risk and Insurance Specialist (**CRIS**) and the Associate in General Insurance (**AINS**) designations.

Printed in the USA
CPSIA information can be obtained
at www.ICGtesting.com
LVHW041030070624
782599LV00001B/83